*Defeating*

# DESTINY

# PICKPOCKETS

ISBN     978-0-9557789-1-9

Printed in the UK.

All Scripture is from the King James Version.

Published by:

Akin-Abraham Productions, 5 Lanridge Road, London SE2 9SJ.


Email the author at:
akinabrahamproductions@yahoo.co.uk

# Table of Contents

Introduction

1. How art thou cut off?....................................7

2. Behold the opportunists!..........................14

3. The "Sandwich" Criminals.......................19

4. Evil Distraction.........................................24

5. Satanic Surveillance.................................30

6. Beware of Witchcraft Manipulation.......35

7. Confront the Destiny Pickpockets.........41

SECTION 2

8. Getting started........................................50

9. Terminate the agenda of your enemies...52

10. Returning Witchcraft Spell.....................57

11. Release me and die.................................62

12. Deliverance from Coffin spirit.......... ....68

13. Returning satanic arrows and bullets....73

14. Disgracing the agenda of the night pickpockets....78

15. Disgracing the agenda of demonic in-laws......... ..85

16. Destroying the agenda of marriage pickpockets. ..90

17. Arresting the reproach of marital delay............. . .95

18. Prayers for favour.................................99

19. I will never beg for bread....................104

20. Barrenness must die.............................109

21. Decreeing Passover over stubborn situations......114

22. Healing prayers for the sick.................119

23. Prayers to fulfil divine agenda............125

# INTRODUCTION

$W$here I grew up as a little child, there was a middle aged woman that had an unusual story to tell and it did not matter to her, whether anyone was ready to listen or not. Anywhere she saw an individual or a group of people standing, she would walk up quietly to them and say, *"I am the wife of Adeoti, I am the wife of Popo and I am the wife of Somolu's dad."* Afterwards she would walk away as quietly as she approached them.

This strange woman would find another individual or group, walk up to them and repeat the same words verbatim:

*"I am the wife of Adeoti, I am the wife of Popo and I am the wife of Somolu's dad."*

This was the woman's only message for everyone. The destiny pickpockets had dealt with her. She had been cursed to display a show of shame. Her decent dressing did not give away her insanity, however she was indeed a mad woman. She had been programmed to tell the whole world about her failed marriages to Adeoti, Popo and to the man widely known as Somolu's dad. Her destiny had been altered.

I counsel you to quickly pray this prayer point. *Any show of shame prepared for me for the future scatter in the name of Jesus.*

This book is specifically written with the inspiration of the Holy Spirit to expose, challenge and destroy the clever, subtle, familiar and yet deadly robber spirit that I have referred to as the destiny pickpocket. I am yet to find a living being that has not been a victim or a dead person that had not been burglarized one way or the other by the destiny pickpocket.

I strongly advise anyone that comes across this book to thoroughly study it and utilise the information properly, for it is by doing so, that one can become a terror to destiny pilferers that come in different disguises to make people's lives miserable.

Also, the prayer segments are to be thoroughly and aggressively prayed, as they are directly designed to deal with various spheres of life that are under the attack of destiny pickpockets. You have not come to this world in vain and you must not go back in vain. If you are not currently fulfilling your divine destiny, then you have found in this book a unique tool for your deliverance.

This is a prayer book relevant for all situations and valid for life.

# 1.

# HOW ART THOU CUT OFF?

$I$t is tragic to be a victim of robbery. I was once been a victim of this crime myself. The thief or thieves had me under surveillance for sometime; and they could not have chosen a better time to strike than when I just bought a number of goods and expensive tools and kept them in my garage. The garage had been empty until then. At night, the enemy struck and took everything that was valuable. I was completely wiped out. This was a calamity! The Bible says, "if the thieves come at night and rob you, what a disaster awaits you. *How art thou cut off?"* The scriptures below show how dangerous the enemy can be. The enemy wants it all!

*"The thief cometh not, but for to steal, and to kill, and to destroy: I am come that they might have life, and that they might have it more abundantly."*

*John 10:10*

*"If thieves came to thee, if robbers by night, (how art thou cut off!) would they not have stolen till they had enough?*

*if the grapegatherers came to thee, would they not leave some grapes?"*

*Obadiah 1:5*

The agenda of the destiny pickpocket is simple; it is to steal the one thing that is most valuable; one's own destiny. This is the divine or predestination of what has been ordained to take place in one's life. It is an appointed or ordained future. Destiny is what God has predetermined you to be and to become, in His divine will. In other words, it is God's providential power to guide our path to walk in the ways He has instructed before we were even born. However, we have the free will of either surrendering all to God for His guidance, or we go about life on our own, thereby making ourselves susceptible to the destiny pickpockets that surround our divine destiny.

In my primary school days one of our literature books contained a story that I still vividly remember. It was about traders in a particular village that had a challenging time dealing with robbers that were constantly ambushing them on their way home at the end of the market days.

The gang of thieves would suddenly spring out from the thick forest by the sides of the only route back to the village from the market, which was a narrow footpath. Brandishing different weapons like clubs and machetes, these bandits were formidable. They had caused so much fear in the hearts of the merchants that nobody dared to oppose these plunderers. Any trader that happened to be unfortunate to be a victim of these rouges always lost the whole day's sale.

One particular day, a man was returning home from the market with his wife; having had a particularly good day at the market. With a lot of money concealed in a cloth pouch inside the man's clothes the last thing they needed was a surprise attack by armed robbers.

Unfortunately, they could see a bunch of men dashing out of the forest and blocking the only footpath. These thieves had in their hands different kinds of weapons and were waving them menacingly with all aggression as they waited for this trader and his wife.

The merchant was gripped with a fear of these men and he began to shake aggressively. He was sweating as he trembled. His feet became jelly and began to give way underneath him. He held onto his wife as if expecting help from her.

The woman surprisingly responded in a thunderous voice that even the robbers who were waiting afar could hear distinctly.

With absolute boldness and wisdom she cried, *"My husband, continue to shake. My husband, continue to tremble. When you shake you kill a thousand and when you tremble you kill ten thousands. My husband, continue to shake and continue to tremble."*

The husband indeed was stricken with fear and could not stop trembling as the wife practically dragged him along. She kept on repeating her words loud and clear.
*"My husband, continue to shake. My husband, continue to tremble. When you shake you kill a thousand and when you tremble you kill ten thousands. My husband, continue to shake and continue to tremble."*

This was a very strange battle cry! The bandits were puzzled by the weird combat shivering stance of the man as well as the woman's odd warfare utterances. They were quick to conclude that it was a mystic opposition, as they thought he only possible explanation to this daring challenge must be that of supernatural powers. How can a man be trembling and yet be killing thousands?

The only option available to this gang of robbers was to flee. They were not prepared to die. They had until then, been having their way without opposition. More peculiar was that, it was not a challenge from able body men, but from a seeming weakling of a man and yet a destroyer warlock.

The woman's wisdom and boldness saved her husband and herself that fateful day. The enemy does not know you, it is what you reveal to him that he will use against you.

Unfortunately, unlike armed robbers, destiny pickpockets pose a different kind of opposition. One requires spiritual discernment and the leading of God to be able to defeat them. They are not as audacious and confrontational; in fact they are subtly and appear harmless. They come as trustworthy as a friend, family, colleague and neighbour; however they aim to rob you completely.

To be pickpocketed is a very personal crime. It is awful losing to a trickster. Your destiny is peculiar and personal! A destiny pickpocket targets your person to violate you. If the wicked had confronted you with a witchcraft horn, you will run for your dear life but if he comes as a friend, mentor or pastor you will embrace him.

It is sad that many godly men and women in the bible failed to fulfil their destiny. They lost it to the master dodger; the devil.

A person can be assigned for greatness by divine purpose, walking in God's blessing and anointing and yet suddenly depart from the course of his destiny, serving himself or succumbing to the will of the enemy and ending up abandoned by God.

It is a tragedy that King Saul, that had this wonderful accolade: Appointed by God, filled by the Holy Spirit, gifted with a spirit of prophecy, destined by God to lead Israel, God was with him; but ended up as a failure. He lived his destiny for a while and ended up fulfilling the satanic desire - prostrating himself before a witch and died in shame.

These words might conveniently have been written on the gravestone of Saul, first king of Israel: *"The man whose destiny was pickpocketed by the witch of Endor."* The sad story of Saul in the bible can be found in the book of 1 Samuel.

Another tragic picture of a man who missed his destiny was Samson. He was a special leader for Israel, whose birth was announced by an angel; filled with the Holy Spirit and prepared to help his people Israel to become a free country. He was born for a purpose, which was to deliver his people Israel from bondage of the Philistines. However, after twenty years of walking in God's calling and having succeeded in exhausting the Philistines and bringing a glimmer of anticipation to his country, Samson began to decline.

He became a carnal man and he lost the respect of his folks. However, these words might also conveniently have been written on his gravestone: *"The man whose destiny was pickpocketed by harlots."* The tragic story of Samson in the bible can be found in the book of Judges.

King Solomon was the wisest, wealthiest and most respected man of his time. His destiny was to rid Israel of idolatry! He started well, walked in his destiny, but he too later missed it! He started walking contrary to his destiny: he became an idolater. He accompanied his many wives to their temples, bowing before heathen idols. Again, these words might also conveniently have been written on his gravestone: *"The man whose destiny was pickpocketed by his many wives and idolatory."* The lamentable story of

Solomon in the bible can be found in the book of 1 Kings Chapters 1-11.

Many Christians are ignorant of the gravity of destiny pickpockets! They let down their guards and dine with the enemies. Sadly, as with physical pickpocketing, which is one of the oldest and most widespread crimes in the world, so it is spiritually. It is a fact that a skilled pickpocket can make off with just as much money as an armed robber, without much danger of confrontation or risk of being identified in a line-up.

Destiny pickpockets are subtle and come in disguise and hence many lives have been destroyed by their secret activities. By the time the victim realizes what has happened, the pickpocket is long gone. When you realise that the enemy of your destiny is a close associate, what do you do?

Also, the destiny's Pickpockets can destroy people's lives even at infancy; you will have to pray for the foundational holes in your destiny to be filled up by the fire of the Holy Ghost in the name of Jesus.

Without mincing words, if you are still living below your divine destiny, unfortunately, the truth is, you have been cut off by satanic pickpockets. *How art thou cut off?*

I counsel you to pray these prayer effectively:

1. *As the Lord God of Israel lives and before whom I stand right now, let the agenda of destiny pickpockets for my destiny scatter in the name of Jesus.*

2. *Every agenda of the enemy to steal, kill and destroy my destiny be wasted in the name of Jesus.*

3. *In the name of Jesus, let every good thing stolen from by life by satanic night robbers be returned to me by fire.*

# 2.

# *BEHOLD THE OPPORTUNISTS!*

Some years back, a friend of mine revealed a shocking story about the Master Pickpocket General Overseer of his former Church! My friend was one of the ministers in the church that was based in the United Kingdom. However, their General Overseer was regular to this particular branch even though he was resident overseas.

Whenever the General Overseer came over to the church he would gather his trusted ministers or ambassadors if you like, together for information about some particular women in the church. One of these faithful ministers was my friend.

This "man of God" would require every detail about these women, what they were going through; their marital status, financial situations, disappointments, appointments, sexual activities if known, past dreams, weaknesses, strengths and so on.

Armed with this information the General Overseer would arrange counselling appointments with them individually in his office. The man would then tell them things about their personal lives that they did not expect a stranger would know. They were shocked that he knew them so well. The women must have felt the way the Samaritan woman at the well felt, when our Lord Jesus Christ revealed deep secrets about her, in John 4:29 *"Come, see a man, which told me all things that ever I did: is not this the Christ?"*

At this point the "Overall Spiritual Leader" of this church would begin his manipulations aiming at sleeping with every counselee. He was indeed a child of the devil with insatiable sexual appetite. Through him many destinies were destroyed including some of his ministers.

However, when his cup was full the Lord struck him with a terrible disease that left him paralysed. The eyes of some of his followers including that of my friend were opened and they then fled the church. This is a typical example of an opportunist pickpocket. *Behold the opportunists!*

Destiny pickpockets (satanic agents), work at various levels in the world. The lowest level is similar to the common pickpockets. **This lowest level is made up of simple opportunists**. They simply seek out people who have left themselves vulnerable. They take advantage of opportunities as they arise. These are exploiters that are aware of the vulnerability and the negligence of their victims. If an ignorant Christian is available for them to manoeuvre out of his or her divine destiny, the opportunist pickpocket will gladly oblige.

Destiny pickpocket opportunists come in various forms: it can be that of master-servant relationship, leader-follower relationship, pastor-congregation, friend-friend relationship and family members' relationships. There is a degree of trust in all these relationships hence there is a huge chance that an ignorant Christian will let down his or her guard. After all, these pickpockets are buddies, comrades, confidants, acquaintances, associates, colleagues, companions, mates, partners, brothers, sisters, accomplice, supporters, sympathizers, well-wishers and generally friendly people.

A married woman who recently joined our church had a hard time shaking off the opportunist destiny pickpocket that was monitoring her life. The pickpocket was her former pastor in her old church.

She had been to see her pastor for prayers and counselling concerning her marriage and the clergyman asked her to give to him her wedding ring. Obediently, she removed her wedding ring and gave it to the man. The pastor then removed his own wedding ring and put it on top of his counselee's wedding ring and began to pray on the rings thereby forming a dangerous covenant with the woman.

The covenant was the beginning of her problems. She was pursued by this man physically and spiritually attempting to sleep with her. He even volunteered to be physically present at the labour room as a spiritual assistant during the birth of the woman's baby! The woman and her husband naively agreed. The pastor, having seen the woman's nakedness was aroused and he intensified his pursuit. This couple had to pray intensively to be delivered from the destiny pickpocket.

Christians, who are unguarded and eat whatever comes their way, will soon eat from the devil's table and will end up in early graves. A Christian brother or sister that is a fornicator or an adulterer might eventually receive a coffin as a birthday gift. It is a fact that there are lots of satanic agents moving about like decent people or like Christians in order to destroy lives.

A mid-thirty, spirit filled female Christian minister was so desperate to get married; she rushed into a relationship with a man that claimed to be a Christian. The supposed Christian Brother put the sister in a family way without getting married, or meeting her parents and any of her relations. It is obvious that there was a satanic agenda in place. A destiny pickpocket was at work. The end of such a relationship has often been a disaster. I have counselled lots of women who had suffered from similar relationships that were founded on deceits.

Many years ago, a colleague of mine once came to work one morning fear stricken. She was in her mid-forties. That fateful day, she came to work looking for support and encouragement because of what she saw in her house earlier that morning.

The woman said, she had walked into her bathroom to take her bath, when she accidentally saw her house help naked with a frightening looking waistband covering her waist and her thighs. Her head suddenly felt huge and heavy and her tongue stuck to the roof of her mouth. She ran out of the bathroom forgetting her bath; she struggled into some clothes and rushed to work.

The maid had been living with my co-worker and her children under the same roof, for a couple of years. This incident answered some mysteries surrounding my friend. She always slept most of the time during office hours even whilst standing! With a broken down marriage and financial difficulties, her children were struggling in school.

Nobody was ready to accompany her to confront the pickpocket in her home and she was not prepared to go back to the house with her children either. It is my prayer that the Lord will open your eyes as you are reading this book, to see the opportunist destiny pickpockets in your portion and also give you the boldness and power to confront them in the name of Jesus. I further pray that you receive, by the Spirit of the Living God, the ability to discern a true friend from satanic opportunists. One must be vigilant, so as not to open one's door to evil agents.

Pray these prayers violently:

1. *As the Lord God of Israel lives and before whom I stand right now, let the agenda of satanic friends in my destiny be wasted in the name of Jesus.*

2. *Any spiritual Lot in my portion, I cast you out in the name of Jesus.*

3. *Satanic exchange in my destiny be reversed by fire in the name of Jesus.*

# 3.

# THE "SANDWICH" CRIMINALS.

*I*f you surround yourself with non-achievers, you will start manifesting in the same anointing and likewise, if the unfriendly friends are your close peers, it is only a matter of time before they destroy you. The devil is a master sandwich criminal. It is unfortunate that many people still fall victim to the guile of the "sandwich" strategy of the enemy.

*"He that walketh with wise men shall be wise: but a companion of fools shall be destroyed."*

*Proverbs 13:20.*

There had not been a more appropriate warning than that of Charlotte Elliot's encouraging hymn *"Christian seek not yet repose"* (1789 - 1871). She warned us Christians, about the danger of letting down our spiritual guard. Miss Elliot's carefree life ended at the age of 30 as she became an invalid and remained so for the remaining 52 years of her life. She began to suffer from a degenerative illness. Depression set in as she became more bedridden for over 50 years. She lost her humour, along with her gift for writing and drawing as death became imminent. She wrote about her physical condition thus:

*My Heavenly Father knows, and He alone, what it is, day after day, and hour after hour, to fight against bodily feelings of almost overpowering weakness and languor and exhaustion, to resolve, as He enables me to do, not to yield to the slothfulness, the depression, the irritability, such as a body causes me to long to indulge, but to rise every morning determined on taking this for my motto, "If any man will come after me, let him deny himself, take up his cross daily, and follow me."*

Miss Elliot wrote about 150 hymns, yet her favourite hymn for me, is the *"Christian seek not yet repose."* From her personal experience, she warned Christians who might assume the state of freedom from storm or disturbance of life. A believer that observes daily spiritual siesta will end up in an early grave. The sandwich criminals are waiting for your unguarded hour, so watch and pray. It is a witchcraft strategy to sponsor unfriendly friends, household wickedness, antagonisms, deadly business rivals, neighbours from hell, unfriendly in-laws, satanic lecturers and parents that are spiritual bats. It is like being compassed about by all these evil agents sharing a common interest, which is to destroy one's destiny. Anywhere a person turns to; he or she will always encounter stiff opposition. It is like being fitted into a tight space, crowded by satanic network. It is a deadly satanic sandwich that must be destroyed.

When an army of unrepentant pursuers are after one's life, the sandwich criminals are in place. One will have to pray them out of one's destiny. Many lives are already crushed to a standstill by these wicked agents. Countless people have been driven from pillar to post seeking deliverance from satanic agents who end up compounding their problems. The destiny mob must be confronted and destroyed through intense fire prayers. It is impossible for lazy Christians to escape the satanic legion if they cannot pray with dedication.

Recently, a young man came to me for counselling, during one of the mid-week church services. He complained about constant spiritual attacks on his business that had brought about an unfavourable financial situation. He also said he was always having strange sensations on his body, before the enemy struck. I gave him some prayer points to pray for 7 successive nights. The man was apparently not used to fire prayers as he enquired from me about how to pray it. I demonstrated to him and he decided to give it a try.

After the first night he called me early in the morning to explain what happened to him the night before. He said he was surprised to find himself vomiting after praying just a few prayers. In fact he said he wanted to stop as he was afraid of the reaction; however he encouraged himself and continued. At the end of the 7 nights, he was surprised to feel the newness in his body and spirit.

He later disclosed the sources of some of his problems. He revealed information to me about a bag he had which contained different evil ingredients like salt, candles, perfumes and so on that he had acquired from evil priests and evil counsellors otherwise known as sandwich criminals that surrounded him as friends.

In the mid nineteen sixties football was about passion and not inspired by large amounts of money. Presently, an average professional footballer earns £100,000 per week or more.

In those days there was a certain young man who was a talented footballer. His destiny was cut short by his own friend; his team mate who played the same wing as him. It was impossible for the fellow team mate to have a chance to play when the young gifted player was still playing. In order for this less skilful player to have the opportunity to secure a regular shirt in the team, he resulted to voodoo. He consulted a herbalist who gave him a charm that he put in one of the soccer boots of the endowed footballer.

The hex in one of the boots gave the young star a large and permanent limp after futile medical treatment. That was the end of his career. The destiny pickpocket or the sandwich criminal had picked his destiny.

Reflecting on the literature written about the Apostle Peter the scripture states he was in the high priest's courtyard the evening Jesus was betrayed. Rather than staying with John, who was also there, Peter tried to hide among the Jews who wanted to kill Jesus. He had chosen to be sandwiched by the very enemies of his destiny. When questioned whether he was Jesus' disciple, Peter denied the Lord, even swearing the third time. Since he chose to be with sinful men, he was tempted and sinned. When we choose evil companions, we will eventually break down and sin and in the same vein when evil agents compass us about we are bound to be destroyed, if we do not know how to deal with the situation. The powerful prayers in this book will provide the solutions in the name of Jesus.

Pray these prayers aggressively:

1. *As the Lord God of Israel lives and before whom I stand right now, I come out of satanic sandwich by fire in the name of Jesus.*

2. *By the power in the fire of the Holy Ghost let the power of every satanic pickpocket in my destiny die in the name of Jesus.*

3. *I cut off any hand of darkness in my portion in the name of Jesus.*

# 4.

# EVIL DISTRACTION.

*J*ust as in a magic show, the major method at work when the destiny pickpockets prepare their attack is distraction. Human beings usually focus their attention on one thing at a time, so if they are given anything interesting to focus on, they will not pay attention to what is of value to them. In the pickpocketing world, distraction can get pretty elaborate. Two members of a team might stage a fight while the third member takes advantage of the inattentive crowd.

The devil is providing many people with pleasure and amusement whilst he is busy stealing their destinies. If one continues to attend senseless parties, it will not be long before being derailed from one's God-given destiny. Demonic parties and baseless ceremonies are on the increase. Some people celebrate their birthdays twice a year, and satanic house warming to trap innocent people. A lot of people are living a life of uncertainty and bewilderment as they have fallen victims to these satanic distractions that have wiped them out completely. Foods and drinks at parties have become satanic baits to witchcraft initiations and dangerous evil seeds plantation.

Wicked poisons are no longer exclusive to evil dreams, as a lot of people are now being poisoned with their eyes wide opened.

It is time to wake up from satanic mystification and perplexity. All the family rituals are demonic; they are geared toward satanic transactions and evil exchange.

On a "candy camera show" that depicted how easy it is to distract lots of people, an actor started by going down on all his fours on the ground searching for nothing. As he continued, the passers-by began to show interest in what the actor appeared to be deeply looking for on the ground. One by one they bent down to help him in looking for whatever he was looking for. And quietly the artist withdrew from searching and left a number of people still searching for nothing. This is how easy the devil distracts people through senseless engagements and appointments.

Many destinies have been destroyed by watching witchcraft films. Unfortunately, the most watched movies in the world are demonic ones, in which they initiate children at a very early age into sorcery. At a tender age they learn how to communicate with the devil or with familiar spirits. In a short time, the souls of such children are sold to Satan. It is a tragedy that even the government finds nothing wrong with these films. I wonder if they will ever link the soaring rate of teenage gun killings and blood thirsty knife-wielding adolescents to these satanic distractions and initiations.

Some youngsters, obviously inspired by satanic shows decided to examine the mystery of witchcraft. They bought different kinds of books on the subject and began a careful and detailed search for information on the subject. On the third night of their research, when they returned to their study, they were shocked by what they saw. The witchcraft books were floating in the air! They quickly abandoned the project. Witchcraft has been repackaged; I pray that the Lord God will open the eyes of His children to see the satanic snares and destructions. If voodoo can be purchased on the internet, there is no limit to the transportation of evil!

A woman had a problem purchasing her own property. She had a good job and she was financially okay to secure a mortgage. However, every effort she made concerning conveyance had failed. Whenever, she was close to closing a deal, it would fall through. It was a terrible and embarrassing failure pattern. She narrated her ordeal to me when she started coming to the church.

This woman became disheartened because her daughter, who had owned her own property for some years, decided to sell it to someone else. The woman thought it rational, for her daughter to consider selling the house to her first, knowing her predicament. She got her worst embarrassment when her daughter refused to sell to her, regardless of how good her offer was.

The woman was convinced she was facing a serious spiritual battle. After powerful deliverance prayers and fasting she continued to search for a property. Just as she was close to closing another deal, she started receiving relentless aggressive phone calls from her people back home in Africa. She refused to answer the calls and I encouraged her to see her purchase through before attending to any calls. To the "Glory of God" she eventually secured her own house. If she had answered those calls, that were indeed calculated evil distractions designed to thwart her breakthrough, she would have failed again. *Evil distractions must be terminated in the name of Jesus.*

Sometimes, the enemy will get close to a person, study his strength and weakness and hence prepare the best way to attack. Just as in the physical, occasionally the pickpockets do not want to distract you from your money; they want to bring your attention to it. For instance, one member of a pickpocket team might cry out "Somebody just stole my wallet!" in a crowded place. The instinctive reaction of most people is to make sure they still have their own wallet and valuables, so they will pat whatever pocket it is in. This therefore makes the pickpockets' job a lot easier as it shows them precisely where to look. The wicked love to get close to people, know their weaknesses before they attack. These are the unfriendly friends or if you like satanic agents.

During one of our church ministrations, I was led by the Holy Spirit to say that a lady had in her possession, a metal wrist bangle. Furthermore, I said that the bangle was given to her as a present and for sometime she had not worn this bracelet. However, the bangle was causing evil distractions that had stagnated her life.

At the end of the service, a young lady came to meet me and said she was the person I referred to during the course of the ministration and that the "evil bangle" belonged to her. It was given to her by her sister in-law. Even though I asked her to bring this bangle to church so as to destroy it, it took her about a month before she brought it. Her enemy did want her to obtain deliverance, so they distracted her from bringing this evil bracelet.

It is amazing how children of God ignorantly and carelessly celebrate satanic revivals. They patronise demonic film shows, buy witchcraft books and attend senseless satanic parties. These people equally celebrate Halloween; engage in activities like ghost trips, demonic outdoor fires (bonfire nights), uniform parties, visiting "haunted places." It is sad that these satanic distractions and snares are celebrated in several parts of the civilised world. The bible warns us about these dangerous covenants with unbelievers:

*"Observe thou that which I command thee this day: behold, I drive out before thee the Amorite, and the Canaanite, and the Hittite, and the Perizzite, and the Hivite, and the Jebusite.*

*Take heed to thyself, lest thou make a covenant with the inhabitants of the land whither thou goest, lest it be for a snare in the midst of thee:*

*But ye shall destroy their altars, break their images, and cut down their groves:*

*For thou shalt worship no other god: for the LORD, whose name is Jealous, is a jealous God:"*

*Exodus 34:11-19*

Will the people of God wake up from spiritual slumber, when their joys have been stolen by sworn enemies and unfriendly friends? Many birthrights have been subtly pickpocketted by household wickedness. Lots of people have no clue about how they come about evil loads and bondages in their lives and regrettably, they have no idea about how to be set free. When the yoke of distractions have robbed you of your joy and happiness you will need to cry out to the Lord in prayers for deliverance. You need peace in your life now and most importantly at old age. The devil must not distract you.

It is time to pray the prayers below with anger in your spirit:

1. *As the Lord God of Israel lives and before whom I stand right now, I command every satanic*

distraction fashioned against my destiny to scatter in the name of Jesus.

2. I refuse to be distracted from my divine destiny in the name of Jesus.

3. Every yoke of evil distraction break by fire in the name of Jesus.

# 5.

## *SATANIC SURVEILLANCE.*

*A*nyone that has ever lived in a country such as Britain and in London in particular will be in a good position to understand what a surveillance society is. With progressively more electronic eyes that are increasingly intruding into private lives and with great impacts on everyday activities. It had been said that new technology and "invisible" techniques are being used to gather a growing amount of information about UK citizens. It is also believed that the level of surveillance will grow even further in the next 10 years!

Spiritually, the enemies of one's goodness take careful consideration to watch one's steps. They can only succeed in people's lives after they had surveyed and understood your weaknesses. When the bible says the devil prowls to and fro seeking a prey to destroy, it is suggesting surveillance, strategies and attacks. One needs to be vigilant to satanic observations.

*"Be sober, be vigilant; because your adversary the devil, as a roaring lion, walketh about, seeking whom he may devour:"*

*1 Peter 5:8*

A lady called me on the phone one afternoon. She had never called me in the afternoon before; it was unusual as she always called in the evening. A strange thing had happened to her. She said she was ironing her clothes the day before and she literally felt someone move behind her, even though she was the only one in the house. Also the same day, she said she had finished frying some meat in the kitchen and had turned off the cooker while the meat was still on the cooker. What alarmed her was the smell of burning meat coming from the kitchen. Something had turned on the cooker!

Further, to confirm her worries, her thirteen-year-old son suddenly decided to vacate his room for the living room. When the mother asked him why he abandoned his room, the young man said *"I feel I'm being watched in the room."*

In the physical, the pickpockets put in a great deal of study at the ATM machines where people withdraw their money. They have to be very observant with eagle's eyes to spy on people's bank cards' pin numbers. Armed with information, they can proceed to the next stage of operation. The ignorant prey in no time will be robbed of his or her hard earned money.

A man was said to have escaped overseas from his mother whom he believed was a witch. In the new country, the Lord had blessed him. He was happily married with children. After many years, he prepared to pay his mother a visit back home in West Africa. At the end of their brief meeting, before he departed, his mother called him to her room to show him something. In her room by the wall was a large mirror. The mother asked her son to take a close look in the mirror. To his amazement he could see his whole family in the living room overseas as they relaxed in their routine watching a programme on the television. In fact the man's dog was also in the picture lying down on the floor.

The witch asked her son, *"Is this not your family that you are hiding from me?"* The man was shocked at the vivid revelation. *"Let me show you something,"* the woman continued. *"Is that your dog in the mirror?"* she asked. The man could barely nod his head for his mouth had dried up in fear and shock. The mother then rendered some incantations against the dog and at that very moment, the dog had a seizure and died. She could easily have killed him or any member of his family as easy as she demonstrated.

Alas, the display showed the extent of satanic surveillance and how the enemy could easily terminate a destiny no matter the distance that one maybe from the danger. One should regularly pray against evil monitoring eyes and mirrors because such shadowing activities eventually lead to evil visitation. One must destroy evil monitors before they perpetrate their wickedness.

While I was writing this book, my family and I visited the home of a couple. They were family friends as well as active ministers in our church. After concluding our church service one Sunday we went to visit them. The wife told us a frightful story that will remain with me for years to come.

Many years ago, she owned a hair dressing salon and employed some workers and apprentices. One day, a strange woman walked into her salon to plait her hair. The competent staffs and apprentices offered to do the job but she rejected the propositions. The woman insisted she wanted only the boss, my friend, to plait her hair. It was not unusual for some customers to be resolute about who they would prefer to weave their hair. Some clients were sensitive about who they allowed to lay hands on their heads simply because they considered it to be the symbol of their destiny and as such, they would not want any evil hand to manipulate their fortune. However, some preferred the expertise of one of the staff and in most cases this was the boss or the manager.

As the client removed her head gear for her hair to be plaited, the owner of the salon was shocked at what the woman revealed. At the centre of her head was a horn about the length of the middle finger! This was an evil manifestation. My friend was shaken but did not display her fright even though she was terror stricken inside. She went on to do the hair trying her best but unsuccessful in covering up the horn with hair. It was a close shave. If she had refused to plait the hair, it could spell a serious spiritual battle for her. On the other hand, plaiting the hair of a demonic visitor could present some repercussion.

About a week afterwards, the woman appeared again at her salon. This strange woman thanked the owner of the salon for her service and maturity the last time and she left. Even to this day the encounter is still a mystery. The long standing problems in my friend's life might or might not be connected with the meeting. Every tree that the Lord God did not plant in her life is currently being hewn out by the power in the name of Jesus.

As you continue reading this book, I pray that every activity of witchcraft powers in your divine destiny will be destroyed in the name of Jesus. Evil eyes monitoring the destiny of the children of God will surely receive blindness by the power in the blood of Jesus.

Pray again like this:

1. *As the Lord God of Israel lives and before whom I stand right now, I arrest and paralyse every enemy of my goodness in the name of Jesus.*

2. *You the powers of the night stealing from me die by fire in the name of Jesus.*

3. *Any mystery surrounding my life that has been the source of my problems be unravelled in the name of Jesus.*

# 6.

## *BEWARE OF WITCHCRAFT MANIPULATION.*

*D*estiny Pickpockets are always coming up with new schemes, one must be prepared. The most seemingly harmless of robbers is likely to be the pickpocket. As undetected shoplifter, the pickpocket gradually drains off his victim. With steady hits, the prey becomes weak and subsequently destroyed. Spiritually, a lot of people are being tricked out of their divine destiny. Perhaps, the closest confidant anyone can have, especially as a Christian is a prayer partner. However, a lady was shocked when it was revealed to her that the witch behind her sufferings in life was the very woman she prayed together with on a regular basis for God to grant them solutions to their problems.

The serpent was a regular visitor to the Garden of Eden. Its presence in their estate was not unusual to Eve. It was easy for her to be manipulated because of the intimacy. The Scripture warns us about the cunning nature of a destiny pickpocket which is similar to the serpent in the "Garden."

*"Now the serpent was more subtil than any beast of the field which the LORD God had made. And he said unto the woman, Yea, hath God said, Ye shall not eat of every tree of the garden?*
*And the woman said unto the serpent, We may eat of the fruit of the trees of the garden:*
*But of the fruit of the tree which is in the midst of the garden, God hath said, Ye shall not eat of it, neither shall ye touch it, lest ye die.*
*And the serpent said unto the woman, Ye shall not surely die:*
*For God doth know that in the day ye eat thereof, then your eyes shall be opened, and ye shall be as gods, knowing good and evil.*
*And when the woman saw that the tree was good for food, and that it was pleasant to the eyes, and a tree to be desired to make one wise, she took of the fruit thereof, and did eat, and gave also unto her husband with her; and he did eat."*

*Genesis 3:1-6*

A lady cried to me sometime ago that her baby sister had taken over the role of the next of kin to their parents. The junior sister had changed all relevant documents to the effect and told her point blank that she was now in charge and that there was nothing the big sister could do about it! This is a higher level of manipulation as it has turned into evil control which is a level of witchcraft. The story of the battle for birthright and fatherly blessing concerning the twin brothers in the bible is a realisation of a destiny pickpocket at work:

*"And it came to pass, as soon as Isaac had made an end of blessing Jacob, and Jacob was yet scarce gone out from the presence of Isaac his father, that Esau his brother came in from his hunting.*

*And he also had made savoury meat, and brought it unto his father, and said unto his father, Let my father arise, and eat of his son's venison, that thy soul may bless me.*

*And Isaac his father said unto him, Who art thou? And he said, I am thy son, thy firstborn Esau.*

*And Isaac trembled very exceedingly, and said, Who? where is he that hath taken venison, and brought it me, and I have eaten of all before thou camest, and have blessed him? yea, and he shall be blessed.*

*And when Esau heard the words of his father, he cried with a great and exceeding bitter cry, and said unto his father, Bless me, even me also, O my father.*

*And he said, Thy brother came with subtilty, and hath taken away thy blessing.*

*And he said, Is not he rightly named Jacob? for he hath supplanted me these two times: he took away my birthright; and, behold, now he hath taken away my blessing. And he said, Hast thou not reserved a blessing for me?"*

*Genesis 27: 30-36*

This man, called Esau had been manipulated twice out of his divine destiny by his own blood brother. His junior twin brother had first taken his birthright by trickery and now his blessing through manipulation; the blessing of the first born from their dying father. It would have been a total tragedy for Esau if his father had no blessing at all reserved for him. However, with the leftover blessing, he continued to live below his divine destiny because of the evil manoeuvre, until he was able to have the dominion to break the yoke from off his neck.

Witchcraft activities have multiplied in the world especially in recent years. These satanic pickpockets have precise goals. The agenda of witchcraft manipulation is to weaken, overpower and destroy the children of the Living God. Some Christians are presently suffering attacks in one form or the other from witchcraft practitioners. It is wise to be familiar with the nature of these attacks so as to overcome them. It is crucial for all serious believers to seek the guidance of the Holy Spirit in whatever decisions they need to make or relationships they are entering into.

Generally, the most heartless of the enemies are the ones that seek to rob gradually. This type of adversary weakens their prey and when defenceless, finally destroys completely. The enemy's strategy and purpose at times could be to weaken us, make us fall behind. This is when prayers become difficult and at this point the foe goes for the kill.

In the Scripture, the Amalekites had the characteristics of Satan and his agents. It was the technique of the Amalekites to attack the weak and the unguarded. As the children of Israel crossed the wilderness, the Amalekites caged in those who fell behind the rest of the camp and destroyed them. As a result of this, Israel was told there would be perpetual war with the Amalekites. The enemies with this kind of wicked operation are indeed dangerous. In fact, Israel's kings were commanded to fight them; they were also commanded to utterly destroy them and not to take any spoil. We have a continuous war against Satan and we cannot take any captives. We need to completely destroy the enemies, leaving no room for retaliations. It is said that the enemy you leave behind today will rise against your destiny.

A woman once spoke to me frankly, about her concern. She said the people around her were only interested in stealing her glory. According to her every good thing her hands began, the enemies stole it. She lost her husband, business, children and even her calling. She had been a victim of witchcraft manipulations. Sorcery is imitation of spiritual power; it is using an evil spirit to control and manipulate lives. The damages done by sorcery are immense in homes, relationships, finances and especially in the lives of young children. Teenage killings are on the increase. The evil spirit behind the gun and knife attacks has to be arrested. It is sad to see lots of lives being wasted to the rampage of destiny destroyers.

Also, these satanic activities are what some people refer to as causing general bad luck, health problems, financial and marital failure. It is as when people think that they are cursed or hexed; it is another height of witchcraft manipulations.

God has given us direct instruction to destroy witchcraft powers completely; the same way he ordered the Israelites to totally annihilate the Amalekites. Every enemy of one's joy has to be completely wiped out.

Pray these prayers to arrest witchcraft manipulations in your life:

1. *As the Lord God of Israel lives and before whom I stand right now, witchcraft manipulations of my life die in the name of Jesus.*

2. *Any power that is stealing from me gradually somersault and die in the name of Jesus.*

3. *Every agenda of destiny pickpocket for my future and that of my family members scatter in the name of Jesus.*

# 7.

## CONFRONT THE DESTINY PICKPOCKETS.

*I* grew up intimidated by an uncle. In actual fact, all my brothers and sisters were equally apprehensive or fearful of this uncle. We were raised up to believe that this man had wicked witchcraft powers. Anytime we saw him afar off coming to our house, every child would run off to hide until he departed. He lived in the village while we lived in the city.

One fateful day, many years later, when we were now grownups and living alone in our family house without our parents, this uncle decided to pay us a visit. We were shocked to see this man. Indeed, he said he came to spend the weekend with us!

Every one of us started making excuses hinting we would not be available that weekend to look after him. We were hoping he would change his mind and return to the village. Unfortunately, he was not be fooled by our obvious pretence; he was determined to stay the weekend.

The problem was how to confront this destiny pickpocket? The best way we knew then was to patronise him. That is a mistake that most people make; patronising the enemy. A sworn adversary can never be appeased. Our friendly gesture was to buy for him some alcoholic drinks. He drank until he was drunk. In his drunken stupor, he brought out from his flowing gown, a very tiny evil horn that he had brought with him to curse us. It took divine intervention of another uncle that was passing by and decided to stop over at that moment. The evil uncle was rigorously begged to give up his evil intention.

Confronting the wicked is a big task. It is not easy to tackle the spiritual destiny pickpockets or the task of having to destroy them completely. Their mode of operation makes it difficult. However, the Spirit of the Living God that reveals the deepest secrets will discern the guise of the devil. The spirit of the destiny pickpocket is generally camouflagic; it is full of disguise. Any power masquerading to harm the children of God shall be disgraced in the name of Jesus.

To a combatant Christian, who is aware that his or her Commander-in Chief is Jehovah, the Man of War, then the agenda of destiny pickpockets will always fail. I said combatant because not all Christians are ready to battle even though the God they believe in, is not a civilian. If the bible says *He is a man of war,* then *He cannot be a civilian.* My years of experience as a Minister of God have revealed to me different kinds of Christians which I have come into contact with. I have taken the time to categorise them.

The first category that I have seen are the ones I referred to as the *Napping Christians.* They are unaware of imminent danger or trouble because they are spiritually asleep. They assume they have heard enough sermons that should last them for their life time. Also, they believe they have prayed enough and that there cannot possibly be anything new about prayers that they have not heard off or prayed before. They therefore, have ceased to grow spiritually. This is a very dangerous position to be in.

The *Reclining Christians* are the ones that take it easy. They lack the zeal of the combatant Christians. This group of persons require lots of encouragements to pray and fellowship with God. They are very quiet spiritually. Just like the previous group, they have readjusted themselves into low class position. They have tailored their lives into accepting stagnancy and reproach. Unfortunately, they have unconsciously customized themselves to what the enemies want them to be.

There is another group that I refer to as the *Lazing Christians*. They lean back. They want to be prayed for. They do not want to put in efforts to change their situation. The people in this group need a lot of begging and persuasions before they attend church services. Eventually, they will be there after a barrage of aggressive invitations from mobile phone text messages and cajoling. Often, the folks in this category sooner or later settle down into shame and poverty. These are individuals who have refashioned themselves into being the hunted and not the hunter. Destiny pickpockets are going to be around for a long time, and there is not much a lazy Christian can do to stop them. They are certainly not a match for the destiny pickpockets.

I have also seen the *Sluggish Christians*. They drag when action is to be taken. They are slowing down, and the enemies are catching up with them. This is the group of unachievers. When a person is slow in taking actions concerning the issues of his or her life, such an individual will end up a failure. When a person has a bad dream that needs quick counter prayers to destroy the completed work of darkness, delay is deadly. Gradually people in this group would be remodelled his into vagabonds by the enemies. It is similar to living without a purpose in life. Satan prefers Christians to stay right where they are, lazy and sluggish, happy to do little and just moderate. These are people that are contented to remain where they are. This again is certainly not a group that can confront the destiny pickpockets.

There are individuals that I refer to as the *Relaxing Christians*. They were once hot and had the enemies in their grip, but lost the authority. These are Christians; once powerful prayer warriors, intercessors and on fire for God. These are former champions of the Gospel of Our Lord Jesus Christ, who are now lukewarm spiritually. Even though this group still see themselves as Christians, the Lord has spewed them out of His mouth because they are neither hot nor cold. Anyone in this group cannot confront the destiny pickpockets.

I call the last group the *Firing Christians*. These are active, vigilant and ready to sacrifice all to succeed. They are the no-nonsense combatant Christians who study the word of God on a regular basis and are always eager to fellowship in the presence of God. The Firing Christians are the prayer warriors who are obedient to the commandments of God. They are the humble giants who have become terrors to the kingdom of darkness. Every Christian must be encouraged to belong to this group in order to overcome the satanic robbers that prowl to steal from them. Every destiny pickpocket has to be confronted and destroyed.

Our Lord Jesus Christ gives us the assurance of victory over the agenda of secret enemies. The plans of masquerading powers shall be exposed. Every child of God is encouraged to be bold and confront the destiny pickpockets. Violent faith, coupled with intense prayers and fasting will destroy the programme of evil powers waiting to steal, kill and destroy the plans of God in people's lives. Jesus specifically gave us authority to drive out evil spirits and to heal every disease and sickness. It is not the portion of a believer to be afraid of the enemies and their deception, because every hidden agenda shall be exposed and disgraced:

*"Fear them not therefore: for there is nothing covered, that shall not be revealed; and hid, that shall not be known."*

*Matthew 10:26*

*"Be strong and of a good courage, fear not, nor be afraid of them: for the LORD thy God, he it is that doth go with thee; he will not fail thee, nor forsake thee."*

*Deuteronomy 31:6*

*"Fear thou not; for I am with thee: be not dismayed; for I am thy God: I will strengthen thee; yea, I will help thee; yea, I will uphold thee with the right hand of my righteousness."*

*Isaiah 41:10*

*"For I the LORD thy God will hold thy right hand, saying unto thee, Fear not; I will help thee."*

*Isaiah 41:13*

By the power of prayer you will recover your destiny! What has the enemies stolen from your life? Is your finance under the attack of the destiny pickpocket? The word of God says you are a tree planted by the rivers of water that is bringing forth fruits in every season. Your source of income should be flowing ceaselessly. The scripture says the young Lions (even in their prime), do lack and suffer hunger, but you cannot lack any good thing because you wait upon the Great Provider. The Psalmist also said he had never seen the righteous beg for bread. If one's finance is under attack or at this moment a person is begging for bread, it is the agenda of destiny pickpocket that is prospering in one's life. There is no situation that cannot be changed through aggressive prayers.

Prayer made the sun to standstill. It will standstill for you and the powers of darkness will not be able to introduce wickedness into your life that will hinder your breakthrough in the name of Jesus.

If marriages, jobs, relationships, health and children are under attack, it is the work of destiny pickpockets. They are the enemies of good things in one's life. By the power of prayers that bring fire from the sky, fire will come down from above and destroy every enemy of joy in your life in the name of Jesus.

There is a caution in the Bible that we must *"Pray without ceasing."* Simply put, the scripture is saying to cease to pray is disastrous. Evil usually happen to those that cease to pray. The enemies of man are ceaseless in doing evil as they do not sleep. It is said that the adversaries of the souls of men do not sleep at all, for they are continuous destiny pickpockets. I pray you will be a ceaseless prayer warrior in the name of Jesus.

You are about to progress to the very essence of this book, which is to destroy the agenda of the devil in different areas of people's lives. The next section contains powerful and aggressive prayers that will defeat the activities of the destiny pickpockets in many finances, homes, marriages and so on. Stubborn situations that have refused to yield will be overturned by the power of aggressive prayers. It is going to challenge rejection, loneliness and poverty. Also, the evil effects of witchcraft activities, lateness in marriages and problems of demonic in-laws shall be destroyed in the name of Jesus.

Pray these three prayer before you go to the prayer section:

1. *As the Lord God of Israel lives and before whom I stand right now, I receive power to confront every enemy of my joy in the name of Jesus.*

2. *Every demonic anointed weapon assigned to destroy me catch fire in the name of Jesus.*

3. *Every battle against my destiny in the heavens, on earth and underneath the earth break up in the name of Jesus.*

# SECTION 2.

# PRAYERS TO DESTROY THE AGENDA OF DESTINY PICKPOCKETS.

## *Getting started:*

You should make this *significant routine* whenever you want to begin any of the prayer segments.

- ✓ Firstly, undergo powerfully, a session of praise and worship that will lift your heart into the happy presence and peace of God. The power of worship will provide the channel for God's power to operate in your circumstance.

- ✓ Secondly, always ask God for forgiveness of the sins in your life. The eyes of the Lord run to and fro throughout the whole earth, to show Himself strong on behalf of those whose hearts are perfect toward Him and not in the interest of a sinner. The prayers will only work for you after you have pleaded for pardon and made a u-turn from any wrongdoing.

- ✓ Thirdly, believe God and thank Him by faith for answers to your petitions.

- ✓ Fourthly, soak yourself and your environment intensely in the blood of Jesus and the fire of the Holy Ghost.

## *Caution:*

Every chosen prayer in this section must be prayed with hostility that is free of sympathy towards the enemy of your destiny, for a minimum of 7 successive nights. For more effective results, the prayers can be prayed for 14 or 21 uninterrupted nights. The prayers must go well beyond the midnight on every occasion.

*Prayer points that order a power, spirit or thing to die are directed to cause expiration of their effects on your life. There is no prayer point directed at personalities.*

This book will transform your fortune forever in the name of Jesus.

# 8.

# TERMINATE THE AGENDA OF YOUR ENEMIES.

These prayers are to cause the enemy of your destiny to be of no effect or of no consequence. It will cause your oppression and the oppressors to cease to exist.

It is a spiritual as well as physical fact that certain things will have to give way for others to materialise. If you do not kill the enemies of your destiny, you will die unfulfilled.

For David to fulfil his destiny he had to eliminate Goliath and Saul was removed for him to be king of Israel.

King Saul of Israel failed to carry out the specific instruction of God to him to completely wipe out the enemies. Thus the remnants that he spared attacked Israel during the time of the Judges and often raided the Israelites' land after they had planted crops, leaving them with nothing.

It is dangerous for anyone not to completely annihilate the enemies when he or she has the opportunity. These prayers are for those who are weary and worn out from apparent unprovoked satanic attacks and are prepared to destroy completely the enemies of their greatness.

The prayers must be prayed with great aggression and determination that will bring sudden turn around to your destiny.

## CONFESS THESE SCRIPTURES:

**1 Samuel 15:2-3:** Thus saith the LORD of hosts, I remember that which Amalek did to Israel, how he laid wait for him in the way, when he came up from Egypt.
3Now go and smite Amalek, and utterly destroy all that they have, and spare them not; but slay both man and woman, infant and suckling, ox and sheep, camel and ass.

**Isaiah 49:25-26:** But thus saith the LORD, Even the captives of the mighty shall be taken away, and the prey of the terrible shall be delivered: for I will contend with him that contendeth with thee, and I will save thy children.
And I will feed them that oppress thee with their own flesh; and they shall be drunken with their own blood, as with sweet wine: and all flesh shall know that I the LORD am thy Saviour and thy Redeemer, the mighty One of Jacob.

## PRAYERS:

1. I receive power to destroy every enemy of my divine destiny in the name of Jesus.
2. I receive power to utterly destroy every power and spirit hindering my joy in the name of Jesus.
3. Whether the enemies like it or not, I am coming out delivered in this prayer session in the name of Jesus.

4. Any personality that has made it his/her business to hinder, me I paralyse you by fire in the name of Jesus.

5. Any evil covenant in my foundation, break in the name of Jesus.

6. Anything belonging to me in the coven of darkness be released in the name of Jesus.

7. Any household wickedness that refuses to let me go, release me and die in the name of Jesus.

8. I come out of any satanic cage in the name of Jesus.

9. Any power drinking the milk and honey of my life, die in the name of Jesus.

10. Any conclusion in the heavens to disgrace me, scatter in the name of Jesus.

11. Satanic rage against my staff of bread, scatter in the name of Jesus.

12. I cancel by fire, witchcraft dreams that are caging my life in the name of Jesus.

13. Afflictions in my body be swallowed by the fire of the Holy Ghost in the name of Jesus.

14. Satanic blanket covering my glory, scatter in the name of Jesus.

15. You the hardship in my foundation, receive deliverance in the name of Jesus.

16. Incantations that had held me captive release me and die in the name of Jesus.

17. Satanic prophesy that holds me captive release me and die in the name of Jesus.

18. Witchcraft powers in charge of my case release me and die in the name of Jesus.

19. Foundational covenant, release me and die in the name of Jesus.

20. Stubborn curses working in my life release me and die in the name of Jesus.
21. Power of failure in my destiny, come out and die in the name of Jesus.
22. You the Goliath of my destiny, your time is up release me and die in the name of Jesus.
23. You the poverty in my foundation release me and die in the name of Jesus.
24. Charms, hexes, jinxes working against my divine destiny, your time is up, die by fire in the name of Jesus.
25. Effects of satanic consumption in the dream release me and die in the name of Jesus.
26. Blood covenant that has refused to let me go, release me and die in the name of Jesus.
27. Powers of my father's house assigned against my life die in the name of Jesus.
28. Powers of my mother's house assigned against my life die in the name of Jesus.
29. Witchcraft gathering against my divine destiny, scatter by fire in the name of Jesus.
30. Anointed tongue speaking against my joy be cut off in the name of Jesus.
31. Idols of my father's house that will not leave me alone die in the name of Jesus.
32. Idols of my mother's house that will not leave me alone die in the name of Jesus.
33. You the power of death and hell in my life release me and die in the name of Jesus.
34. Eaters of flesh and drinkers of blood I am not your candidate, eat your own flesh and drink your own blood in the name of Jesus.
35. Every coffin spirit assigned against me scatter in the name of Jesus.

36. Every graveyard spirit waiting to swallow me up die in the name of Jesus.
37. I separate myself from any spirit of Lot limiting my divine destiny in the name of Jesus.
38. Any household strife in my portion, scatter in the name of Jesus.
39. I drop by fire, any strange load in my destiny in the name of Jesus.
40. I look northward and I claim my divine portion in the name of Jesus.
41. I look southward and I claim my divine portion in the name of Jesus.
42. I look eastward and I claim my divine portion in the name of Jesus.
43. I look westward and I claim my divine portion in the name of Jesus.
44. I believe every prayer point that I have prayed will bring abundant testimonies in the name of Jesus.
45. Begin to thank the Lord by faith for empowering you to destroy the enemies of your divine destiny.

# 9.

# *RETURNING WITCHCRAFT SPELL.*

Anyone that is serious about freedom from witchcraft mechanism will have to pray these prayers with holy anger and desperation.

Many lives are under witchcraft manipulation, intimidation and domination. There is hardly anyone that is free from witchcraft terrorism.

These prayers will particularly destroy witchcraft spells and incantations working against your destiny. Every hex or curse overriding your life will be destroyed.

The number one enemy of one's destiny is the power of witchcraft. Exodus 22:18 says *"Thou shalt not suffer a witch to live."*

**CONFESS THESE SCRIPTURES:**

**Micah 5:12:** And I will cut off witchcrafts out of thine hand; and thou shalt have no more soothsayers:

**Psalm 125:1:** They that trust in the LORD shall be as mount Zion, which cannot be removed, but abideth for ever.

**Psalm 35:8:** Let destruction come upon him at unawares; and let his net that he hath hid catch himself: into that very destruction let him fall.

**Isaiah 50:7:** For the Lord GOD will help me; therefore shall I not be confounded: therefore have I set my face like a flint, and I know that I shall not be ashamed.

**Numbers 23:23:** Surely there is no enchantment against Jacob, neither is there any divination against Israel: according to this time it shall be said of Jacob and of Israel, What hath God wrought!

As I go into this prayer session, I believe I will come out victorious for greater is He that is in me than the host of witchcraft.

It is written, he that leadeth into captivity shall go into captivity: he that killeth with the sword must be killed with the sword. By faith, every witchcraft oppression in my life must die in this prayer session in the name of Jesus.

It is also written, Behold, I lay in Zion a stumbling stone and a rock of offence: and whosoever believeth on Him shall not be ashamed. I believe in the word of God and I will not be ashamed in the name of Jesus.

Every hex, jinx, charm, curse and spell of witchcraft must go back to the owners as I pray in the name of Jesus.

**PRAYERS:**

1. Lord as I go into this prayer session, I believe you will help me and I shall not be confounded in the name of Jesus.
2. Father Lord, my eyes are focused on you and I know that I shall not be ashamed in the name of Jesus.
3. Lord Jesus let my story change at the end of this prayer session in the name of Jesus.
4. Let the power of God in me destroy the evil powers around me in the name of Jesus.
5. Every enchantment and divination against my life backfire in the name of Jesus.
6. Let destruction come unawares upon witchcraft priests assigned against me in the name of Jesus.
7. Let the evil net that the enemies has hidden to catch me catch the enemies in the name of Jesus.
8. Let my detractors fall into the very destruction they have prepared for me in the name of Jesus.
9. Every witchcraft power that compasses me about be cut off in the name of Jesus.
10. Witchcraft powers assigned to move me into destruction die by fire in the name of Jesus.
11. Any satanic judgement against my life in the heavenlies, scatter in the name of Jesus.
12. Every satanic completion in heaven against my life scatter by fire in the name of Jesus.
13. Every satanic completion in the body of water against my life scatter in the name of Jesus.
14. Every evil completion in my foundation working against me die in the name of Jesus.
15. You the seven elders judging my life at the gate somersault and die in the name of Jesus.
16. Any seven evil powers united against my joy, what are you waiting for, scatter in the name of Jesus.

17. Every seven ingredients used against my life be roasted in the name of Jesus.
18. Any seven elders that had ever ministered evil against my life die in the name of Jesus.
    *Genesis 4:15 says that anyone who killed Cain would pay for it seven times over.*
19. Seven fold judgement of God come upon any power tormenting my life in the name of Jesus.
20. Any wickedness completed against my life, scatter in the name of Jesus.
21. Any completed work of darkness against my life, die in the name of Jesus.
22. Evil caldron cooking my affairs, scatter by fire in the name of Jesus.
23. Evil agreement against my destiny, scatter by fire in the name of Jesus.
24. Any evil power in my foundation that wants to disgrace me die in the name of Jesus.
25. Any strange god that is bent on wasting my life, die in the name of Jesus.
26. I refuse to labour in vain in the name of Jesus.
27. Any power that wants me to live my old age in shame and loneliness die in the name of Jesus.
28. Anointing of bad ending die in the name of Jesus.
29. You the king Uzziah in my life die, king of glory arise in the name of Jesus.
30. Anything in my foundation waiting for my day of glory to destroy me catch fire in the name of Jesus.
31. I refuse to end up a failure in the name of Jesus.
32. Every power assigned against my breakthroughs, your time is up, therefore die in the name of Jesus.
33. Witchcraft spells, jinxes, hexes and charms working in my foundation backfire in the name of Jesus.

34. Witchcraft spells, jinxes, hexes and charms working against my progress backfire in the name of Jesus.
35. Witchcraft spells, jinxes, hexes and charms working against my divine inheritance backfire in the name of Jesus.
36. I fire back every arrow of laziness and poverty in the name of Jesus.
37. I fire back every arrow of stagnancy in the name of Jesus.
38. I fire back every arrow of failure at the edge of breakthrough in the name of Jesus.
39. I fire back every arrow of rejection and loneliness in the name of Jesus.
40. I fire back every arrow of non-achievement in the name of Jesus.
41. I fire back every evil arrow of the night and that of the noonday in the name of Jesus.
42. I thank God for setting me free by the power in the blood of Jesus.

# 10.

# RELEASE ME AND DIE.

It is always a difficult exercise for a prisoner to free himself or herself. If you want the household wickedness tormenting your life and caging your destiny to die, then you must pray this prayer with full concentration and aggression.

You will have to pray as much as Paul and Silas in Acts 16:25-29:

"And at midnight Paul and Silas prayed, and sang praises unto God: and the prisoners heard them.

And suddenly there was a great earthquake, so that the foundations of the prison were shaken: and immediately all the doors were opened, and every one's bands were loosed.

And the keeper of the prison awaking out of his sleep, and seeing the prison doors open, he drew out his sword, and would have killed himself, supposing that the prisoners had been fled.

But Paul cried with a loud voice, saying, Do thyself no harm: for we are all here.

Then he called for a light, and sprang in, and came trembling, and fell down before Paul and Silas,"

Evil satanic embargo or padlock affecting your life will scatter and the powers of darkness will release you and die if you believe in your right as a child of God.

If you look at yourself right now and see that all your efforts and inputs in life have always failed to obtain success, you need to pray the payers of "Release me and die". If instead of going forward you keep going backward, you need these prayers.

The prayers are going to provoke dumbfounding breakthroughs, make sure you are not distracted.

## CONFESS THESE SCRIPTURES:

**Isaiah 6:1:** In the year that king Uzziah died I saw also the Lord sitting upon a throne, high and lifted up, and his train filled the temple.

**Philippians 2:9-10:** Wherefore God also hath highly exalted him, and given him a name which is above every name: That at the name of Jesus every knee should bow, of things in heaven, and things in earth, and things under the earth;

**Exodus 12:12:** For I will pass through the land of Egypt this night, and will smite all the firstborn in the land of Egypt, both man and beast; and against all the gods of Egypt I will execute judgment: I am the LORD.

## PRAYERS:

1. Every "Cain" in my household, loose your power over my life, in the name of Jesus.
2. You my "Cain" die, in the name of Jesus.

3. You the "Herod", in my life die, in the name of Jesus.
4. Tap root of infirmities in my life, die, in the name of Jesus.
5. You the fear of tomorrow in my life die in the name of Jesus.
6. Satanic programme into the moon and the star against me, I dismantle you in the name of Jesus.
7. Lay your hands on your head and say: Boldness, Power, Prosperity and Purity, fall upon me now, in the name of Jesus.
8. Any evil thing programmed into this year against me, I dismantle you, in the name of Jesus.
9. Any sickness programmed into my life, by fire by force, fall down and die, in the name of Jesus.
10. Every evil thing programmed into my life, fall down and die, in the name of Jesus.
11. You my life be disconnected from every spirit of failure, in Jesus' name.
12. My life will not attract failure and disappointment, in the name of Jesus.
13. Any enemy that does not want to let me go be buried alive, in the name of Jesus.
14. Evil bird assigned against my life, fall down and die, in the name of Jesus.
15. Every foundational barrier, limiting my progress crumble in the name of Jesus.
16. Any curse in my family line affecting my life break in the name of Jesus.
17. Any mistake I have made in the past affecting my present be overturned by the blood of Jesus.
18. Every curse and limitation of my place of birth and country affecting my life break and loose your hold in the name of Jesus.

19. Every deeply entrenched problem dry up from the root in the name of Jesus.
20. Every arrow of death assigned against me die in the name of Jesus.
21. O Lord, restore back onto me, everything I have lost to destiny pickpockets in the name of Jesus.
22. Every tree of sorrow in my foundation, be uprooted in the name of Jesus.

**Lay your right hand on your head as you pray the next 3 prayers:**

23. I fire back every arrow of the enemy, in the name of Jesus.
24. Every power that has stolen from my destiny return it and die in the name of Jesus.
25. My glory, arise and shine in the name of Jesus.
26. Every good thing I have lost through satanic distraction and deception be returned by fire in the name of Jesus.
27. I refuse to roll over for the devil; I wake up and pursue my pursuers in the name of Jesus.
28. I recover by fire my joy stored in the second heavens, in the name of Jesus.
29. You the atmosphere hear the word of the Living God; vomit my destiny in the name of Jesus.
30. Evil trees harbouring my greatness scatter by fire in the name of Jesus.
31. Any satanic kingdom and authority in the water, wasting my life scatter in the name of Jesus.
32. O Earth! Hear the word of the living God vomit me by fire in the name of Jesus.
33. Evil rituals at crossroads against my life backfire in the name of Jesus.
34. Any human being that has stolen from me vomit it by fire in the name of Jesus.

35. I receive power to overcome every long standing problem in my life in the name of Jesus.
36. I cancel evil effects of curses in my life in the name of Jesus.
37. I break every secret curse upon my life in the name of Jesus.
38. I break and cancel every curse issued by satanic ministers in the name of Jesus.
39. I break and cancel every curse emanating from evil prophecies in the name of Jesus.
40. Any curse I have brought upon myself as a result of my sin, blood of Jesus break it in the name of Jesus.
41. I break every evil yoke fashioned against my destiny in the name of Jesus.
42. I break loose from any curse and yoke brought upon me by any past generation in the name of Jesus.
43. Any evil maintenance officer, assigned against my life, receive spiritual paralysis, in the name of Jesus.
44. I silence any evil utterances against my life in the name of Jesus.
45. O Lord arise and bring final solution to all my stubborn situations in the name of Jesus.
46. Let all satanic kingdoms working against me fail in the name of Jesus.
47. Every tree of sorrow in my life, wither from the root in the name of Jesus.
48. I paralyse everyone behind the extension and expansion of my problems in the name of Jesus.
49. I loose myself from every dark spirit in the name of Jesus.

50. Let the backbone of my stubborn pursuers and strongman break in the name of Jesus.
51. Let the blood and strength of my stubborn pursuers dry up in the name of Jesus.
52. Begin to thank the Lord for your breakthrough in the name of Jesus.

# 11.

# DELIVERANCE FROM COFFIN SPIRITS.

God has the power to set free, even those that are already appointed to death. Psalm 102:20. *"To hear the groaning of the prisoner; to loose those that are appointed to death"*

In as much as you are still walking on the surface of the earth, you have to pray against any death sentence in your life. You must be delivered from the coffin spirit in the name of Jesus.

If you sometimes see yourself in the dream; with dead relatives or losing jobs, investments and business this section is for you.

It is a fact that many people had dead relatives who had formed covenants with them consciously and unconsciously when they were alive. Such covenants will still be binding, unless you break them by the power in the name of Jesus.

You will have to make the confessions loud and clear and pray these prayers very well for you to live to fulfil your God given destiny.

**CONFESS THESE CRIPTURES:**

**Psalm 118:17:** I shall not die, but live, and declare the works of the LORD.

**Hebrews 5:7:** Who in the days of his flesh, when he had offered up prayers and supplications with strong crying and tears unto him that was able to save him from death, and was heard in that he feared;

## PRAYERS:

1. I cover myself with the blood of Jesus and the fire of the Holy Ghost in the name of Jesus.
2. I believe the Lord has blessed me with long life and I will not die before my time in the name of Jesus.
3. It is written, no evil shall befall me at anytime therefore anyone and any power sponsoring evil against me shall be wasted in the name of Jesus.
4. Powers of my father's house assigned to waste my life die in the name of Jesus.
5. Powers of my mother's house assigned to destroy me die by fire in the name of Jesus.
6. Every strongman assigned against my destiny, die in the name of Jesus.
7. Every witchcraft gathering against my life, scatter and die in the name of Jesus.
8. Evil tongues anointed to curse me, catch fire in the name of Jesus.
9. Any satanic priest, ministering at any evil altar against my life somersault and die in the name of Jesus.
10. Evil words spoken against my destiny be cancelled by fire in the name of Jesus.

11. You the idol of my father's house that has refused to let me go you are a liar; die in the name of Jesus.
12. You the idol of my mother's house that refused to let me go, be consumed by fire in the name of Jesus.
13. Let the mouths of the eaters of flesh and drinkers of blood receive the fire of God in the name of Jesus.
14. Any power preparing coffin for my life, enter your coffin and die in the name of Jesus.
15. Evil programme in the heavens against my life scatter in the name of Jesus.
16. Every power contesting for my breakthroughs, die in the name of Jesus.
17. Evil decisions taken against my life by witchcraft spirits, be wasted in the name of Jesus.
18. Every conscious and unconscious covenant with the dead, break! in the name of Jesus.
19. Every gate of death and hell opened against me, CLOSE! in the name of Jesus.
20. Every infirmity in my life receive the fire of deliverance in the name of Jesus.
21. Any man or woman prophesying against my destiny, run mad in the name of Jesus.
22. You the satanic minister calling my name for evil, receive the judgement fire of God in the name of Jesus.
23. Any evil gathering against my life what are you waiting for, scatter in the name of Jesus.
24. Tongue of viper cursing my destiny, be roasted in the name of Jesus.
25. I prophesy against any contrary power assigned against my joy and I command you to be

swallowed by the raging fire of God in the name of Jesus.

26. Any personality that enjoys seeing my tears, be disgraced in the name of Jesus.

27. You my star, break loose from evil cage in the name of Jesus.

28. I am the head I am not the tail, any power that wants me to die as a tail, die in the name of Jesus.

29. Any cooperation in the heavens to waste my life be wasted in the name of Jesus.

30. Every satanic sentence against my destiny, die in the name of Jesus.

31. You my picture in the hands of evil ministers receive the fire of deliverance and I command the evil ministers to die in the name of Jesus.

32. I command my finances to receive deliverance from every power of darkness that is determined to waste my labour in the name of Jesus.

33. Every sting of death in my life be destroyed by the fire of the Holy Ghost in the name of Jesus.

34. Any sin in my life that is making me an easy target for the enemy die in the name of Jesus.

35. Evil plantation in my life, my body is the temple of God therefore come out and die in the name of Jesus.

36. I am the carrier of the Most High God I refuse to carry evil load, therefore any strange load in my life, I drop you by fire in the name of Jesus.

37. Holy Ghost fire, unmask any personality masquerading against me and disgrace them in the name of Jesus.

38. Every good thing stolen from my life by household wickedness be returned by fire by force in the name of Jesus.

39. You the hunter of good things in my life, die suddenly in the name of Jesus.
40. I receive power to feast in the presence of my enemies in the name of Jesus.
41. Every good thing that is dead in my life, be revived in the name of Jesus.
42. I shall not die before my time in the name of Jesus.
43. Let the judgement of God come upon my detractors in the name of Jesus.
44. It is written, with long life will my God satisfy me therefore I shall not die before my time in the name of Jesus.
45. Every conscious and unconscious covenant with any dead relative, break in the name of Jesus.
46. Arrows of death and hell in my life backfire in the name of Jesus.
47. I believe by faith, that all the prayers that I have prayed in this segment shall bring forth testimonies in the name of Jesus.
48. This year, whether the enemies like it or not, I shall celebrate in the name of Jesus.

# 12.

# RETURNING SATANIC ARROWS AND BULLETS.

A number of people have received arrows and bullets in the dream and woke up feeling the effect physically. Also, there have been substantial cases of Christians who are on fire that have received similar attacks and the arrows and bullets backfired.

Satanic arrows come also as food consumption in the dream, sex and evil visitation etc. Many people have died as a result of these satanic missiles.

It is possible to receive the arrows and bullets of the enemies and die instantly and it is also possible to still be moving about. However, such an arrow recipient, if still living, will gradually deteriorate physically and spiritually until the enemy pulls the final trigger.

You must not wait for the enemy to finish you up. It is scriptural to return satanic arrows and bullets. The arrow of the vagabond has to be returned, if your life has no head way and you have been stagnant for too long you will have to pray seriously.

It is time to fire back arrows of lateness in any department of your life.

## CONFESS THESE SCRIPTURES:

**Revelation 13:10:** He that leadeth into captivity shall go into captivity: he that killeth with the sword must be killed with the sword. Here is the patience and the faith of the saints.

**Psalm 34:21:** Evil shall slay the wicked: and they that hate the righteous shall be desolate.

**Deuteronomy 7:15:** And the LORD will take away from thee all sickness, and will put none of the evil diseases of Egypt, which thou knowest, upon thee; but will lay them upon all them that hate thee.

**Jeremiah 1:19:** And they shall fight against thee; but they shall not prevail against thee; for I am with thee, saith the LORD, to deliver thee.

## PRAYERS:

1. I return by fire evil arrows and bullets that the enemy fired into my mind and thought in the name of Jesus.
2. Every arrow of failure fired into my head go back to your sender in the name of Jesus.
3. Any satanic judgement against my life in the heavens, scatter in the name of Jesus.
4. Every satanic completion in the body of water against my life, scatter in the name of Jesus.
5. You the vessel of my life become too hot for strangers to inhabit in the name of Jesus.
6. I vomit by fire, every food that I have taken from the table of the devil in the name of Jesus.

7. Anything in me cooperating with the devil, die in the name of Jesus.
8. Every property of darkness in my possession, I drop you in the name of Jesus.
9. You the Achan in my life come out and die in the name of Jesus.
10. You the Achan in my household come out and die in the name of Jesus.
11. Any evil power, demanding my cooperation die in the name of Jesus.
12. Every satanic bank account in my name be roasted in the name of Jesus.
13. I withdraw my name from every satanic payroll in the name of Jesus.
14. I refuse to humour the oppressor in the name of Jesus.
15. Any power that is rejoicing at my misfortune die in the name of Jesus.
16. I waste every power wasting my life in the name of Jesus.
17. You the spirit of Edom competing with the Spirit of God in my life die in the name of Jesus.
18. You the power of the spirit of the bond woman making me to sweat in vain fall down and die in the name of Jesus.
19. You the house of war warring with my house of peace be wasted in the name of Jesus.
20. You my Israel arise defeat your Esau in the name of Jesus.
21. Any righteous verdict prospering in my life be overruled by the blood of Jesus.
22. Every foundational barrier, limiting my progress crumble in the name of Jesus.

23. Any curse in my family line affecting my life break in the name of Jesus.
24. Any mistake I have made in the past affecting my present be overturned by the blood of Jesus.
25. Every curse and limitation of my place of birth and country affecting my life break in the name of Jesus.
26. Every deeply entrenched problem in my life dry up from the root in the name of Jesus.
27. Every arrow of death assigned against me die in the name of Jesus.
28. Every house of shame constructed for me, scatter in the name of Jesus.
29. Every power dragging my progress in the ground, your time is up die in the name of Jesus.
30. Every evil power of my father's house assigned against my breakthrough die in the name of Jesus.
31. Every evil power of my mother's house assigned against my breakthrough die in the name of Jesus.
32. Every arrow of wickedness fired into my life in the dream backfire in the name of Jesus.
33. Every bullet of the enemy in my vessel come out and locate your owner in the name of Jesus.
34. Every owner of evil load in my life, carry your load in the name of Jesus.
35. Every satanic completion in heaven against my life, scatter by fire in the name of Jesus.
36. Any power that is waiting to celebrate my disgrace, die in the name of Jesus.
37. Any power assigned to waste my life, be wasted in the name of Jesus.
38. Evil arrows and bullets fired into my staff of bread backfire in the name of Jesus.

39. I claim divine protection by the blood of Jesus from every arrow of the enemy in the name of Jesus.
40. Arrows sent into my life through evil incantations backfire in the name of Jesus.
41. The blood of Jesus has set me free from all satanic arrows and bullets in the name of Jesus.
42. I claim my divine breakthroughs in this prayer segment in the name of Jesus.

# 13.

# DISGRACING THE AGENDA OF THE NIGHT PICKPOCKETS.

The hour of the night should be the period of sleep however, the bible says while men slept, his enemy came and sowed tares among the wheat, and went his way.

1Thessalonians 5:5 says *"For you are all children of light, children of the day. We are not of the night or of the darkness"*.

The scriptures below will show you how dangerous the night time is. Many destinies have been swapped, truncated and terminated. For some people, it has been a time of evil visitation. In fact many are afraid to go to sleep.

Job 7:3-4:  So am I made to possess months of vanity, and wearisome nights are appointed to me. When I lie down, I say, When shall I arise, and the night be gone? and I am full of tossings to and fro unto the dawning of the day.

Job 24:14-15: The murderer rising with the light killeth the poor and needy, and in the night is as a thief. The eye also of the adulterer waiteth for the twilight, saying, No eye shall see me: and disguiseth his face.

Exodus 12:12: For I will pass through the land of Egypt this night, and will smite all the firstborn in the land of Egypt, both man and beast; and against all the gods of Egypt I will execute judgment: I am the LORD.

2 Kings 19:35: And it came to pass that night, that the angel of the LORD went out, and smote in the camp of the Assyrians an hundred fourscore and five thousand: and when they arose early in the morning, behold, they were all dead corpses.

Daniel 5:30: In that night was Belshazzar the king of the Chaldeans slain.

This is not a joking matter. If you can overcome the powers of the night and disgrace the night pickpockets of your destiny, you will surely have a fulfilled life.

This prayer segment is to be done only during the hours of the night. The prayers should begin anytime from 12 midnight for the minimum of 7 uninterrupted nights.

**CONFESS THESE SCRIPTURES:**

**Psalm 68:1:** Let God arise, let his enemies be scattered: let them also that hate him flee before him.

**Psalm 91: 1-16:** "He that dwelleth in the secret place of the most High shall abide under the shadow of the Almighty.

I will say of the LORD, He is my refuge and my fortress: my God; in him will I trust.

Surely he shall deliver thee from the snare of the fowler, and from the noisome pestilence.

He shall cover thee with his feathers, and under his wings shalt thou trust: his truth shall be thy shield and buckler.

Thou shalt not be afraid for the terror by night; nor for the arrow that flieth by day;

Nor for the pestilence that walketh in darkness; nor for the destruction that wasteth at noonday.

A thousand shall fall at thy side, and ten thousand at thy right hand; but it shall not come nigh thee.

Only with thine eyes shalt thou behold and see the reward of the wicked.

Because thou hast made the LORD, which is my refuge, even the most High, thy habitation;

There shall no evil befall thee, neither shall any plague come nigh thy dwelling.

For he shall give his angels charge over thee, to keep thee in all thy ways.

They shall bear thee up in their hands, lest thou dash thy foot against a stone.

Thou shalt tread upon the lion and adder: the young lion and the dragon shalt thou trample under feet.

Because he hath set his love upon me, therefore will I deliver him: I will set him on high, because he hath known my name.

He shall call upon me, and I will answer him: I will be with him in trouble; I will deliver him, and honour him.

With long life will I satisfy him, and shew him my salvation."

## PRAYERS:

1. Father Lord as I begin these prayers, I confess by faith that I dwell in your secret place and abide under your shadows in the name of Jesus.
2. Father Lord, be my refuge and my fortress as I go into this night battle in the name of Jesus.
3. Father Lord, cover me with your feathers and let me remain under your wings in the name of Jesus.
4. With boldness I declare that I am not afraid of the terror by night nor for the arrows that fly by day because you protect me in the name of Jesus.
5. I cover myself with the blood of Jesus against the pestilence that walks in darkness in the name of Jesus.
6. Fire of God surround and protect me from the night criminals in the name of Jesus.
7. I receive power to disgrace every night criminal harassing my life in the name of Jesus.

8. Father Lord arise and disgrace every enemy of my peace in the name of Jesus.
9. The snares of the fowler opened against my life scatter in the name of Jesus.
10. By fire by force every witchcraft power working against my destiny fall by my side and die in the name of Jesus.
11. Every plan of the household wickedness against my life shall not materialise in the name of Jesus.
12. Father Lord release your angels of death upon every night criminal working against my life in the name of Jesus.
13. I trample under my feet every night lion and adder harassing my life and I command you to die in the name of Jesus.
14. You the night dragons assigned against my life fall down and die in the name of Jesus.
15. Father let you covenant of peace and long life be renewed in my life in the name of Jesus.
16. Completed works of darkness fashioned against my life scatter in the name of Jesus.
17. You the night, hear the word of the living God fight against every enemy of my peace in the name of Jesus.
18. You the powers of the night hear the word of the Living God; vomit every good thing that has been stolen from me in the name of Jesus.
19. Finger of God, rewind every witchcraft dream affecting my life and cancel them in the name of Jesus.
20. Every dream of failure die in the name of Jesus.
21. Every dream of backwardness die in the name of Jesus.

22. Every dream designed to bring me back to square one die in the name of Jesus.

23. By fire by force every night ritual fashioned against my life backfire in the name of Jesus.

24. Satanic priests keeping vigils for my sake be disgraced by fire in the name of Jesus.

25. Any power that has sown tares in the field of my life somersault and die in the name of Jesus.

26. Every tare in the field of my life come out and die in the name of Jesus.

27. Evil visitations in the dream working against my life backfire in the name of Jesus.

28. Evil eyes that see in the darkness monitoring my life for evil catch fire in the name of Jesus.

29. Satanic night collectors amassing the honey of my life, I command the earth to open up and swallow you in the name of Jesus.

30. Conscious and unconscious satanic initiations at night be destroyed by the blood of Jesus.

31. Conscious and unconscious evil dedications at night be destroyed by the blood of Jesus.

32. Evil night sacrifices that had closed up my heavens scatter in the name of Jesus.

33. Every witchcraft meeting summoned for my sake scatter in the name of Jesus.

34. Any hand of darkness in my portion, wither by fire in the name of Jesus.

35. Satanic hands that have ever touched my destiny waste away in the name of Jesus.

36. Let the strength of the strongman assigned to waste my life fail in the name of Jesus.

37. Every good dream that has not materialised in my life, by the power of the Holy Ghost, begin to manifest in the name of Jesus.

38. Every power masquerading to steal from me, fall down and die in the name of Jesus.
39. Holy Ghost power, unmask the night criminals and disgrace them in the name of Jesus.
40. Light of God disperse the darkness in my portion in the name of Jesus.
41. From now henceforth, I declare by faith that I am untouchable to the powers of the night and I rule over every power of the night delegated against my destiny in the name of Jesus.

## *14.*

## *DISGRACING THE AGENDA OF DEMONIC IN-LAWS.*

In most cases when a man and a woman marry they assume that all their troubles are now over. They seem to have opened the heavenly gate, and passed through its portals into joy unspeakable and everlasting. Together they will resist the world as they are sheltered in their comfort den. Then suddenly, the household wickedness rise up and every good thing in the marriage is under attack.

The battle of demonic in-laws is a sensitive and hot battle. It is even more delicate if a spouse is on the side of his own family against the other.

If the problem in one's marriage is largely due to the activities of unfriendly in-laws, one will have to pray these prayers aggressively.

You will have to pray this on your own away from your spouse if he or she is not of the same opinion with you. The Lord will see you through in Jesus name.

**CONFESS THESE SCRIPTURES:**

**Deut. 28:7:** The Lord shall cause thine enemies that rise up against thee to be smitten before thy face, they shall come out against thee one way and flee before thee seven ways.

**Isaiah 8:10:** Take counsel together, and it shall come to nought; speak the word, and it shall not stand: for God is with us.

**Isaiah 54:17:** No weapon that is formed against thee shall prosper; and every tongue that shall rise against thee in judgment thou shalt condemn. This is the heritage of the servants of the LORD, and their righteousness is of me, saith the LORD.

## PRAYERS:

1. I soak the foundation of my marriage in the blood of Jesus.
2. Fire of God, go the very beginning of my marriage and purge out evil influence in the name of Jesus.
3. Any agreements in the heavenlies against the joy of my marriage scatter in the name of Jesus.
4. Any strange leg that has found its way into my marriage I cut you off in the name of Jesus.
5. Any man or woman assigned against my marriage, be disgraced in the name of Jesus.
6. Lord Jesus, visit the hearts of all my in-laws and control them to my favour in the name of Jesus.
7. Any witchcraft power, that is using my in-laws against me die in the name of Jesus.
8. Any evil power strengthening my in-laws against me, fall down and die in the name of Jesus.

9. Anything in my life that is making me a target for demonic in-laws, come out and die in the name of Jesus.

10. I render null and void any satanic counsel between my in-laws and my spouse in the name of Jesus.

11. You my (husband or wife) reject satanic counsel in the name of Jesus.

12. I claim marital bliss in the name of Jesus.

13. Every spirit of marriage destruction in the foundation of my spouse's life, fall down and die in the name of Jesus.

14. Every power assigned to put my marriage asunder fail, in the name of Jesus.

15. You the evil spiritual head of my spouse's house, release my marriage and die in the name of Jesus.

16. Every evil proclamation by my in-law against my marriage be rendered null and void in the name of Jesus.

17. Anything done in the dark against my marital bliss, backfire in the name of Jesus.

18. Every power that reports my marriage in the witchcraft meeting be exposed and be disgraced in the name of Jesus.

19. Caldron of darkness prepared against my marriage break in the name of Jesus.

20. Every in-law with serpentine tongue your prayer over my marriage will not be answered in the name of Jesus.

21. Every evil covenant made with placenta of my (husband/wife) by my in-law, break in the name of Jesus.

22. Evil tree assigned against my spouse from his /her place of birth receive the fire of God and burn to ashes in the name of Jesus.

23. Every curse pronounced by my in-law over my marriage be converted to blessing in the name of Jesus.

24. Every evil connection between my spouse and my in-laws break in the name of Jesus.

25. Every in-law with evil imagination for my marriage be exposed and be disgraced in the name of Jesus.

26. Power of God, incubate my marriage in the name of Jesus.

27. Foundational error in my marriage be destroyed in the name of Jesus.

28. Every unfriendly friend and in-law be exposed and be disgraced in the name of Jesus.

29. Demonic wedding engagements affecting my marriage be destroyed by the blood of Jesus.

30. Any mark of hatred in my life be washed off by the blood of Jesus.

31. Any power using my in-laws against me, die in the name of Jesus.

32. You my home become too hot for demonic in-laws in the name of Jesus.

33. Any strange leg in my marriage be cut off in the name of Jesus.

34. I cover my body with the blood of Jesus for favour and promotion in the name of Jesus.

35. You my husband/wife, you will not reject the counsel of God for our marriage in the name of Jesus.

36. You the evil power using my husband/wife against me fall down and die in the name of Jesus.

37. Every divine blessing of marriage envelope my marriage in the name of Jesus.

38. I thank God for dispatching demonic in-laws from my marriage in the name of Jesus.
39. I thank God for bringing back joy into my marriage in the name of Jesus.
40. I thank God for the joy of my marriage shall not die in the name of Jesus.

# 15.

# DESTROYING THE AGENDA OF MARRIAGE PICKPOCKETS.

With the rate of divorce on a staggering increase, Christians should not be ignorant of satanic expectation for marriages. Many Christian couples have already been separated and many more will still break-up unless people learn to pray to keep the union God has given them. It is a tragedy when a Christian marriage lasts for just some few hours! At least I know of one.

Satan's very first job was to attack the maiden marriage instituted by God. If you are experiencing attacks in your marriage you need to pray these prayers. When the man or woman that used to love and care for you suddenly does not want to see your face around, you have prayers to undergo.

With the slightest sign of disagreement in a marriage Christians should learn to pray. When your partner starts keeping late nights, drinking alcohol and keeping strange friends, it is the warning signal. That which the Lord has joined together let not man put asunder.

**CONFESS THESE SCRIPTURES:**

**Matthew 19:3-6:** The Pharisees also came unto him, tempting him, and saying unto him, Is it lawful for a man to put away his wife for every cause?

And he answered and said unto them, Have ye not read, that he which made them at the beginning made them male and female,

And said, For this cause shall a man leave father and mother, and shall cleave to his wife: and they twain shall be one flesh?

Wherefore they are no more twain, but one flesh. What therefore God hath joined together, let not man put asunder.

**Genesis 2:24-25:** Therefore shall a man leave his father and his mother, and shall cleave unto his wife: and they shall be one flesh. And they were both naked, the man and his wife, and were not ashamed.

**Hebrews 13:4:** Marriage is honourable in all, and the bed undefiled: but whoremongers and adulterers God will judge.

**Ecclesiastes 4: 9-12:** Two are better than one; because they have a good reward for their labour. For if they fall, the one will lift up his fellow: but woe to him that is alone when he falleth; for he hath not another to help him up. Again, if two lie together, then they have heat: but how can one be warm alone? And if one prevail against him, two shall withstand him; and a threefold cord is not quickly broken.

## PRAYERS:

1. The word of God says and I believe that what God has joined together, let not man put asunder in the name of Jesus.

2. Any man or woman that has made it his /her business to hinder me be disgraced in the name of Jesus.

3. Negative marital patterns from my parents, my marriage is not your candidate in the name of Jesus.

4. The powers of my father's house and my mother's house harassing my marriage die in the name of Jesus.

5. Any power from my spouse's family that wants our marriage to fail, die in the name of Jesus.

6. Any personality that has eaten my food and is still bent on destroying my marriage be disgraced in the name of Jesus.

7. You the spirit husband or spirit wife claiming the right to my marriage somersault and die in the name of Jesus.

8. Blood of Jesus renew my love in my spouse's heart in the name of Jesus.

9. You the strongman assigned against my glory, it is your time to expire therefore die in the name of Jesus.

10. Glory of my marriage manifest in the name of Jesus.

11. Father Lord, release your angels of death into the camps of my enemies in the name of Jesus.

12. Every agenda of marriage breakers for my marriage scatter in the name of Jesus.

13. Any dangerous covenant in my marriage break in the name of Jesus.

14. You the in-law with evil agenda for my marriage be exposed and be disgraced in the name of Jesus.

15. Satanic power controlling the mind of my spouse against me die in the name of Jesus.

16. Holy Ghost fire trouble the power that troubles the joy of my marriage in the name of Jesus.

17. Holy Ghost power, trouble the powers assigned against my glory in the name of Jesus.

18. Holy Ghost power trouble evil in-laws in my marriage to the point of surrender in the name of Jesus.

19. You my glory reject bewitchment in the name of Jesus.

20. Anything in my life attracting demonic friends and in-laws, come out and die in the name of Jesus.

21. Every rage of the wicked against my happiness, scatter in the name of Jesus.

22. Evil marriage counsellors in my life be disgraced in the name of Jesus.

23. Demonic covenants during marriage engagement break and shake off in the name of Jesus.

24. Every hunter spirit tracking my life for evil fall down and die in the name of Jesus.

25. Witchcraft powers assigned against my progress fall down and die in the name of Jesus.

26. Anything that I did not buy that I am paying for what are you waiting for die in the name of Jesus.

27. Evil salary advance disgracing my divine destiny die in the name of Jesus.

28. Hardships in my foundation as a result of satanic initiations be destroyed by fire in the name of Jesus.

29. Every enemy that I left behind that is rising up against my marriage fall down and die in the name of Jesus.
30. Every enemy that I left behind that is determined to cast me out of my divine inheritance somersault and die in the name of Jesus.
31. Every dangerous covenant affecting the joy of my marriage break in the name of Jesus.
32. Any unfulfilled promise that I made and is now hunting me die in the name of Jesus.
33. Every blood covenant that I had left behind and is now affecting my marriage be destroyed by the blood of Jesus.
34. Strange legs in my marriage catch fire in the name of Jesus.
35. You the serpent in my marriage be roasted in the name of Jesus.
36. Any evil in my house be dispersed by fire in the name of Jesus.
37. Wrong foundations in my marriage be repaired in the name of Jesus.
38. I receive divine power to rescue my marriage from the claws of marriage breakers in the name of Jesus.
39. I receive divine fire to burn to ashes every enemy of my marriage in the name of Jesus.
40. I receive the anointing to pursue and recover everything that had been stolen from my marriage in the name of Jesus.
41. I claim by faith, divine restoration of my marriage from the powers of the night and the powers of the day in the name of Jesus.
42. I am testifying by faith to the awesome power of God in my marriage in the name of Jesus.

# 16.

# ARRESTING THE REPROACH OF MARITAL DELAY.

It is said that almost two-thirds of women in their twenties do agree that it is not unusual for a woman to remain unmarried into her 30s. However, for a man or a woman that is well over 30, it is becoming a reproach to be single. It is a satanic desire to deprive lots of people from getting married.

It is strategically wise for Satan to prevent a marriage from happening than having to destroy it.

If you are of a marriageable age and all your mates have been married you owe yourself the duty to destroy that reproach. The Lord will deliver you from every evil work of the enemy of your destiny in the name of Jesus.

**CONFESS THESE SCRIPTURES:**

**Isaiah 49:24-25:** Shall the prey be taken from the mighty, or the lawful captive delivered? But thus saith the LORD, Even the captives of the mighty shall be taken away, and the prey of the terrible shall be delivered: for I will contend with him that contendeth with thee, and I will save thy children.

**2 Timothy 4:18:** And the Lord shall deliver me from every evil work, and will preserve me unto his heavenly kingdom: to whom be glory for ever and ever. Amen.

**Colossians 1:13:** Who hath delivered us from the power of darkness, and hath translated us into the kingdom of his dear Son:

**Galatians 6:17:** From henceforth let no man trouble me: for I bear in my body the marks of the Lord Jesus.

## PRAYERS:

1. In this prayer session, I am coming out with outstanding testimonies in the name of Jesus.
2. Lord, reveal to me the secrets of my life in the name of Jesus.
3. Any power reversing the promises of God in my life it your time to expire in the name of Jesus.
4. Fire of God burn my reproach to ashes in the name of Jesus.
5. Anywhere the bone of my bone and the flesh of my flesh is, as I go into these prayers, arise and locate me in the name of Jesus.
6. Any hex, jinx, charm and spell working against my settling down in marriage be destroyed by the blood of Jesus.
7. Conscious and unconscious anti-marriage covenants break in the name of Jesus.
8. Any wedding done in the spiritual realm that is

working against my marriage be destroyed in the name of Jesus.

9. Spiritual wedding gown delaying my marriage catch fire in the name of Jesus.

10. Spiritual wedding certificates working against my marriage be roasted by fire in the name of Jesus.

11. Spiritual wedding ring standing against my marriage be destroyed by fire in the name of Jesus.

12. Spiritual marriage witnesses hindering my settling down in marriage die in the name of Jesus.

13. You the spirit husband/wife hindering my marriage fall down and die in the name of Jesus.

14. Any conscious and unconscious blood covenant standing against my marriage break and lose your hold in the name of Jesus.

15. Every enemy that I had left behind hindering my joy fall down and die in the name of Jesus.

16. Family pattern of lateness in marriage, I am no longer your candidate; release me by fire in the name of Jesus.

17. Every foundational barrier, limiting my progress crumble in the name of Jesus.

18. Any curse in my family line affecting my life break in the name of Jesus.

19. Household wickedness holding back my marriage, scatter and die in the name of Jesus.

20. You the yoke of collective captivity working in my life break by fire in the name of Jesus.

21. You the yoke of witchcraft manipulations break by fire in the name of Jesus.

22. Fire of God; mount a road block against evil visitations of spirit husband/wife in the dream in the name of Jesus.

23. Any deposit of spirit husband/wife in my vessel

come out and die in the name of Jesus.

24. Every anti-marriage forces working in my foundation die in the name of Jesus.
25. Any mistake I have made in the past affecting my present be overturned by the blood of Jesus.
26. Every curse and limitation of my place of birth and country affecting my life break.
27. Every deeply entrenched problem in my life dry up from the root in the name of Jesus.
28. Fire of God, separate my life from any man or woman that will disappoint me in the name of Jesus.
29. Yoke of unprofitable delay break by fire in the name of Jesus.
30. Satanic road block mounted against my settling down scatter by fire in the name of Jesus.
31. Any satanic wall standing between me and my divine partner crumble in the name of Jesus.
32. Evil voice saying no to marriage, be silenced in the name of Jesus.
33. I jump out of my parents; my parents jump out of me in the name of Jesus.
34. Marriage delay as a result of what my parents had done die in the name of Jesus.
35. I break the yoke of any man or woman who had jokingly claimed to me my husband/wife in the past in the name of Jesus.
36. I declare by faith that I am free and available for marriage in the name of Jesus.
37. I believe God that I have settled down and His peace reigns in my life in the name of Jesus.
38. I believe God for my victory in the name of Jesus.

# *17.*

## *PRAYERS FOR FAVOUR.*

Often times, the unbelievers talk about people being in the right place at the right time, luck and unmerited favour; what they are as a matter of fact talking about is divine favour.

It is dangerous for any Christian to ignore the importance of divine favour in everyday life. The bible says in Colossians 1:16 that *"for the sake of our Lord Jesus heaven and earth was created."* If indeed you are complete in Jesus, who is complete in the Father, then your life must be blessed and highly favoured both in heaven and on earth as they were created for your benefit.

You can pray these prayers when you have an interview or appointment for which you require approval or success. When you pray the prayers, God will command men for your sake, people will bend over backwards to favour you.

When you are expecting a decision on a matter or require angelic blessings in any department of your life you will have to pray the prayers very well. If the heart of the king is in the hands of our Lord, then He will control the hearts of your superiors to favour you in Jesus name.

**Confess this aloud as you go into the prayers:** *For my sake heaven and earth were created, therefore I receive divine favour in the heavens and in the earth. Men and women shall favour me. The winds of God shall carry my divine helpers unto me in the name of Jesus. The heart of anyone that will determine my future shall be controlled to favour me in the name of Jesus. I am blessed and highly favoured in the name of Jesus.*

## CONFESS THESE SCRIPTURES:

**Colossians 1:16-17:** For by him all things were created: things in heaven and on earth, visible and invisible, whether thrones or powers or rulers or authorities; all things were created by him and for him. He is before all things, and in him all things hold together.

**Ecclesiastes 9:11:** I returned, and saw under the sun, that the race is not to the swift, nor the battle to the strong, neither yet bread to the wise, nor yet riches to men of understanding, nor yet favour to men of skill; but time and chance happeneth to them all.

**Proverbs 21:1:** The king's heart is in the hand of the LORD, as the rivers of water: he turneth it whithersoever he will.

**Job 10:12:** You gave me life and showed me kindness, and in your providence watched over my spirit.

**Psalm 75:6-7:** For promotion cometh neither from the east, nor from the west, nor from the south. But God is the judge: he putteth down one, and setteth up another.

**Deuteronomy 28:13:** And the LORD shall make thee the head, and not the tail; and thou shalt be above only, and thou shalt not be beneath; if that thou hearken unto the commandments of the LORD thy God, which I command thee this day, to observe and to do them:

## PRAYERS:

1. Anything in my life chasing away my divine helpers come out and die in the name of Jesus.
2. Thou power of God, command everything to turn around for my favour in the name of Jesus.
3. Every garment of reproach and disfavour upon my life, catch fire and roast to ashes in the name of Jesus.
4. Holy Ghost fire arise and connect me to my divine helpers in the name of Jesus.
5. Door of divine favour open unto me by fire in the name of Jesus.
6. Strongman of impossibility, loose your hold upon my destiny in the name of Jesus.
7. God my Father, let men bend over backwards to bless me in the name of Jesus.
8. Thou power of God command men on my behalf in the name of Jesus.
9. Any man or woman that God wants to use to promote me, appear and locate me by fire in the name of Jesus.
10. Every glory paralyser assigned against my life somersault and die in the name of Jesus.
11. Special announcement, powers of my father's house my life is not for sale therefore release me and die in the name of Jesus.

12. I pull down every wall of partition standing between me and my divine helpers in the name of Jesus.

13. As wax melts before the fire, every wicked opposition in my life melt away in the name of Jesus.

14. Any power chasing away my divine helpers, fall down and die in the name of Jesus.

15. I command my divine helpers to break loose from any evil chain tying them down and I command them to locate me in the name of Jesus.

16. I jump out from the furnace of reproach and failure in the name of Jesus.

17. Every darkness around me that is preventing my divine favour, disappear by fire in the name of Jesus.

18. Lion of Judah arise and pursue affliction out of my life in the name of Jesus.

19. Oppression of my father's house die in the name of Jesus.

20. Every opposition to my breakthrough be silenced permanently in the name of Jesus.

21. Any power struggling to suppress my glory, die by fire in the name of Jesus.

22. You my life attract divine favour in the name of Jesus.

23. Rod of the Living God, swallow the rod of the wicked in my life in the name of Jesus.

24. Fire of the Living God repair the vehicle of my destiny in the name of Jesus.

25. You the vehicle of my destiny, you will not leave me behind in the name of Jesus.

26. By fire by force, I enter into my season of divine favour now in the name of Jesus.

27. Glory of my divine destiny arise and shine in the name of Jesus.
28. God arise and restore me to your original design for my life in the name of Jesus.
29. My Father and my God let your presence shake the foundation of my problems and destroy them in the name of Jesus.
30. You my portion, receive total deliverance from the rod of the wicked in the name of Jesus.
31. Every arrow of limitation, fired into my destiny, go back to your sender in the name of Jesus.
32. Every satanic embargo placed upon my destiny be lifted by fire in the name of Jesus.
33. I put on the garment of favour in the name of Jesus.
34. Lord let men and women bend over backwards to favour me anywhere I go in the name of Jesus.
35. At the end of this prayer session, I claim my divine favour in the name of Jesus.
36. By faith, I thank God for the baptism of divine favour in the name of Jesus.

# 18.

# I WILL NEVER BEG FOR BREAD.

It is the will of God for His children to prosper even as their souls prosper. Therefore, anyone whose life is not fulfilling this scripture will need to cry out to the Lord in the prayers in this segment.

If you are in any form of financial debt or you do not, at this moment in time, have a job and stable financial income these deliverance prayers are for you.

Also, if people are owing you money and they are dragging their feet in paying back, you must know that your money is tied down in the kingdom of darkness.

There are loads of treasures in the kingdom of darkness that are meant for the children of the kingdom of God. The bible says the eyes of the Lord are upon the righteous, and His ears are open unto his cry. Also, when the righteous cries, the Lord hears, and delivers him out of all his troubles.

Do not joke with these prayers and by the power in the word of God, your life will never remain the same in the name of Jesus.

## CONFESS THESE SCRIPTURES:

**Jeremiah 17:7-8:** Blessed is the man that trusteth in the LORD, and whose hope the LORD is. For he shall be as a tree planted by the waters, and that spreadeth out her roots by the river, and shall not see when heat cometh, but her leaf shall be green; and shall not be careful in the year of drought, neither shall cease from yielding fruit.

**Psalm 34:10:** The young lions do lack, and suffer hunger: but they that seek the LORD shall not want any good thing.

**3 John 1:2:** Beloved, I wish above all things that thou mayest prosper and be in health, even as thy soul prospereth.

**Isaiah 58:11:** And the LORD shall guide thee continually, and satisfy thy soul in drought, and make fat thy bones: and thou shalt be like a watered garden, and like a spring of water, whose waters fail not.

**Isaiah 45:3:** And I will give thee the treasures of darkness, and hidden riches of secret places, that thou mayest know that I, the LORD, which call thee by thy name, am the God of Israel.

**1 Samuel 2:7-8:** The LORD maketh poor, and maketh rich: he bringeth low, and lifteth up. He raiseth up the poor out of the dust, and lifteth up the beggar from the dunghill, to set them among princes, and to make them inherit the throne of glory: for the pillars of the earth are the LORD's, and he hath set the world upon them.

There is no limit to how long you will have to pray these prayers even when your life begin to experience the abundant blessings of God.

## PRAYERS:

1.  I surrender completely my finances, business, work and monetary issues to the capable hands of God in the name of Jesus.
2.  I refuse to be bothered about where my income will be coming from because I serve THE GREAT PROVIDER in the name of Jesus.
3.  Father Lord, you are my source of abundant living and I put my trust in you in the name of Jesus.
4.  Holy Spirit, guide me and multiply my blessings in the name of Jesus.
5.  Father Lord let your wisdom fill me with prosperity ideas that will promote my life in the name of Jesus.
6.  My debts belong to my saviour; He is more than able to pay them in the name of Jesus.
7.  Every negative thought and fear about money die in the name of Jesus.
8.  The word of God says it is impossible for the righteous to beg for bread therefore any power that wants me to beg for bread shall be disgraced in the name of Jesus.
9.  Even when the strong lack and suffer hunger, because I wait upon the Lord I will never lack any good thing in the name of Jesus.

10. I am a tree planted by the water and any power assigned to transplant me, die in the name of Jesus.

11. Any satanic gateman in charge of my open heaven somersault and die in the name of Jesus.

12. I am the head and not the tail therefore any power that wants me to die as a tail die in the name of Jesus.

13. Witchcraft powers stealing from me die in the name of Jesus.

14. Any power drinking the milk and honey of my life die by fire in the name of Jesus.

15. Jesus died for me, His blood touched the earth and subdued it and therefore I claim my dues in this land in the name of Jesus.

16. You my divine helpers, wherever you are, locate me now in the name of Jesus.

17. Anointing to excel fall upon me in the name of Jesus.

18. O earth, open up and swallow all the enemies of my prosperity in the name of Jesus.

19. Any power from my father's house sitting upon my wealth be unseated by the fire of the Holy Ghost in the name of Jesus.

20. Anything programmed into the heavenlies against my financial breakthrough, be dismantled by the blood of Jesus.

21. O God arise and empower me to prosper and make wealth in the name of Jesus.

22. Every garment of poverty upon my life, I tear you off by fire in the name of Jesus.

23. O Lord, put upon me the garment of prosperity in the name of Jesus.

24. Any ancestral power crying against my prosperity, be silenced by the blood of Jesus.

25. I break loose from every inherited yoke of poverty in the name of Jesus.

26. Poverty of my father's house, my life is not your candidate, therefore release me and die.

27. Every agenda of the thief for my finances shall be disgraced in the name of Jesus.

28. Father Lord, grant me wealth so that I can enrich the lives of people around me in the name of Jesus.

29. Satanic handshakes that are stealing from me be destroyed by the blood of Jesus.

30. The wealth of the Gentiles are stored for me therefore I receive divine direction to locate them in the name of Jesus.

31. I dip my hands into the milk and honey of this nation in the name of Jesus.

32. Men and women will bend over backward to favour me in the name of Jesus.

33. Anointing to reap where I have not sown fall upon me in the name of Jesus.

34. Holy Spirit, hold me by the hand and lead me to my divine breakthroughs in the name of Jesus.

35. Father Lord, I know and I believe you want me to prosper in everything I do in the name of Jesus.

36. I know and I believe that witchcraft powers and household wickedness can no longer steal from me in the name of Jesus.

37. I am grateful to God for all that I now have in the name of Jesus.

# *19.*

# *BARRENNESS MUST DIE.*

As we find in the Bible, examples of people who have been barren and without physical children, so is the same with some people today. However, it is a great joy to know that God helped them to overcome their barrenness, and He is still in the same business of destroying this kind of reproach.

It is important to discern the cause of barrenness. That is, is it God-allowed or devil-driven? God may allow us to experience barrenness as a judgment and curse for sin. In some cases in the bible, fruitfulness was considered to be the result of blessing while barrenness was viewed as a judgment of God or a withholding of blessing.

The barrenness of Michal was as a result of sin, while that of Sarah, Rebekah, Rachel, Manoah's wife, Hannah and Elizabeth were not.

Therefore if the cause of barrenness is due to sin, we need to ask God to point out specific sins in our lives that have resulted into infertility, so that we will be able to deal with them.

The prayers in this section will destroy barrenness that is as a result of the devil's work. All the obstacles in your way of fruitfulness will be destroyed in the name of Jesus. However, you must be determined and desperate in your desire as Hannah and you must be ready to declare death on your barrenness with the genuine desire of Rachel. *Gen 30:1: And when Rachel saw that she bare Jacob no children, Rachel envied her sister; and said unto Jacob, Give me children, or else I die.*

For the miracle of God to appear in one's life, faith is required. Sarah was way past the child-bearing age, yet God changed her situation. You will have to devote specific number of nights to thoroughly pray these prayers.

## CONFESS THESE SCRIPTURES.

**Genesis 30:22-23:** And God remembered Rachel, and God hearkened to her, and opened her womb. And she conceived, and bare a son; and said, God hath taken away my reproach:

**Luke 1:25:** Thus hath the Lord dealt with me in the days wherein he looked on me, to take away my reproach among men.

**Genesis 25:21:** And Isaac intreated the LORD for his wife, because she was barren: and the LORD was intreated of him, and Rebekah his wife conceived.

**Deuteronomy 7:14:** Thou shalt be blessed above all people: there shall not be male or female barren among you, or among your cattle.

**Exodus 23:26:** There shall nothing cast their young, nor be barren, in thy land: the number of thy days I will fulfil.

**Isaiah 54:1-3:** Sing, O barren, thou that didst not bear; break forth into singing, and cry aloud, thou that didst not travail with child: for more are the children of the desolate than the children of the married wife, saith the LORD.
Enlarge the place of thy tent, and let them stretch forth the curtains of thine habitations: spare not, lengthen thy cords, and strengthen thy stakes;
For thou shalt break forth on the right hand and on the left; and thy seed shall inherit the Gentiles, and make the desolate cities to be inhabited.

## PRAYERS:

1. Any defect in my instrument of reproduction, be corrected by the blood of Jesus.
2. Anything in my body that hinders conception come out with your entire root in the name of Jesus.
3. I command the heat or cold drying up my seed to disappear in the name of Jesus.
4. Anything that makes me less of a woman/man, die in the name of Jesus.
5. Any power hindering me from carrying pregnancy to full term die in the name of Jesus.
6. Obstructions to conception scatter in the name of Jesus.
7. Any abnormality in my ovulation/sperm count be destroyed in the name of Jesus.
8. Fire of the Holy Ghost; strengthen my womb to carry my joy in the name of Jesus.
9. Witchcraft powers that want me to die barren; it is your time to die in the name of Jesus.
10. The failure and reproach in my marriage be destroyed by the fire of the Holy Ghost in the name

of Jesus.

11. Negative statistics that make me a disadvantage to child bearing be overturned in the name of Jesus.

12. Satanic prophesies hindering my joy die by fire in the name of Jesus.

13. Sexually transmitted diseases standing against my fruitfulness dry up in the name of Jesus.

14. Powers of my father's house that do not want me to prosper fall down and die in the name of Jesus.

15. Powers of my mother's house that do not want me to prosper fall down and die in the name of Jesus.

16. I disown any children that are attached to me in the spirit realm standing against my physical manifestations in the name of Jesus.

17. Any wickedness completed against my life scatter in the name of Jesus.

18. I refuse to die without my fruits and I will not die before my time in the name of Jesus.

19. Evil caldron cooking my affairs, scatter by fire in the name of Jesus.

20. Every organ in my body functioning below standard, receive the touch of fire of the Holy Ghost in the name of Jesus.

21. Evil agreement against my destiny, scatter by fire in the name of Jesus.

22. Unfavourable clinical prophesies about my body be overturned in the name of Jesus.

23. Any evil power in my foundation that wants to disgrace me, die in the name of Jesus.

24. The curse of barrenness in my foundation, break in the name of Jesus.

25. Any power that wants me to live my old age in shame and loneliness die in the name of Jesus.

26. You the God that remembered Rachel and opened her womb, happen in my life in the name of Jesus.
27. Anointing of bad ending die in the name of Jesus.
28. You the God that took away the reproach of Rebecca, take away my reproach in the name of Jesus.
29. You the king Uzziah in my marriage die, King of Glory arise in the name of Jesus.
30. Completed works of darkness during the hours of the night working against the promises of God in my life die in the name of Jesus.
31. I claim the word of God that says there shall not be male or female barren among my family in the name of Jesus.
32. Anything in my foundation waiting for my day of glory to destroy me catch fire in the name of Jesus.
33. Stubborn yoke of collective captivity break in the name of Jesus.
34. Witchcraft afflictions die in the name of Jesus.
35. I refuse to end up a failure in the name of Jesus.
36. Let the creative power of Him that created the heavens and the earth change my situation in the name of Jesus.
37. By faith I declare my story has changed in the name of Jesus.
38. By faith with my own hands I carry my own children in the name of Jesus.
39. By faith barrenness has died in my life to the glory of God in the name of Jesus.
40. I thank God for answered prayers.

# 20.

# DECREEING PASSOVER OVER STUBBORN SITUATIONS.

The prayers in this segment are created with the power of the Holy Spirit to destroy unyielding conditions. When a circumstance refuses to change after you have fasted, prayed or even done deliverance, then your final option is to decree a Passover over the problem.

Pharaoh, the slave master, had no option but to release the children of God from slavery in Egypt when the captives decreed the Passover. It was the final plague that the Lord released upon the oppressors.

If a problem is typical or of a strong and stubborn nature, one will need to decree Passover aggressively over the situation. When people around you are testifying to the power of God in their lives and you as a Christian are struggling at the tail position, you need these prayers. When the situation in one's life has become a reproach, then it is Passover time!

With the spirit of "enough is enough" stubborn situations in marriage, business, family, finances, health, career, examination, status, job, calling and so on will have no option but to give way when you pray these prayers in the name of Jesus.

## CONFESS THESE SCRIPTURES:

**Obadiah 1:3-4:** The pride of thine heart hath deceived thee, thou that dwellest in the clefts of the rock, whose habitation is high; that saith in his heart, Who shall bring me down to the ground?
Though thou exalt thyself as the eagle, and though thou set thy nest among the stars, thence will I bring thee down, saith the LORD.

**Isaiah 33:1:** Woe to thee that spoilest, and thou wast not spoiled; and dealest treacherously, and they dealt not treacherously with thee! when thou shalt cease to spoil, thou shalt be spoiled; and when thou shalt make an end to deal treacherously, they shall deal treacherously with thee.

**Isaiah 8:9-10:** Associate yourselves, O ye people, and ye shall be broken in pieces; and give ear, all ye of far countries: gird yourselves, and ye shall be broken in pieces; gird yourselves, and ye shall be broken in pieces.
Take counsel together, and it shall come to nought; speak the word, and it shall not stand: for God is with us.

**Isaiah 50:7:** For the Lord GOD will help me; therefore shall I not be confounded: therefore have I set my face like a flint, and I know that I shall not be ashamed.

**Exodus 11:1:** And the LORD said unto Moses, Yet will I bring one plague more upon Pharaoh, and upon Egypt; afterwards he will let you go hence: when he shall let you go, he shall surely thrust you out hence altogether.

## PRAYERS:

1. I claim the victory of Passover event over every stubborn situation in my life as I go into these prayers in the name of Jesus.
2. I cover myself with the blood of Jesus until the morning of my Passover in the name of Jesus.
3. Every Pharaoh that has refused to let me go I declare your expiry as I go into my prayers in the name of Jesus.
4. I shut myself up in the blood of Jesus, O Lord release your angels of death for my sake against my enemies in the name of Jesus.
5. The God of Passover set me free from any hardship in my foundation in the name of Jesus.
6. O Lord release your angels of death into the camps of witchcraft powers assigned against my life in the name of Jesus.

**Cry out the next 7 prayers with destructive force and expectations:**

7. I decree Passover over evil vows against my excellence and distinction and I command them to expire in the name of Jesus
8. I decree Passover over stagnancy and I command you to die in the name of Jesus.
9. I decree Passover over witchcraft activities in my life and I command you to die in the name of Jesus.
10. I decree Passover over stubborn pursuers in my life and I command you to die in the name of Jesus.
11. I decree Passover over stubborn bondage in my life in the name of Jesus.
12. I decree Passover over every power establishing failure, backwardness and demotion in my life and I command you to die in the name of Jesus.

13. I decree Passover over every ancestral door-keeper blocking my breakthroughs and I command you to expire in the name of Jesus.
**Pray the remaining prayers with greater aggression:**
14. The agenda of wasters in my life be wasted in the name of Jesus.
15. By the power in the blood of Jesus, you the hardships in my foundation scatter in the name of Jesus.
16. Every power contesting against my breakthroughs, die in the name of Jesus.
17. Evil decisions taken against my life by witchcraft spirits be wasted in the name of Jesus.
18. Every foundational barrier limiting my progress, crumble by the power of Passover in the name of Jesus.
19. Every conscious and unconscious covenant with the dead, break in the name of Jesus.
20. Every gate of death and hell opened against me scatter in the name of Jesus.
21. Any curse in my family line affecting my life it is your time to expire in the name of Jesus.
22. Any mistake I have made in the past affecting my present be overturned by the blood of Jesus in the name of Jesus.
23. Thou power of Passover destroy every curse and limitation of my place of birth and country affecting my life in the name of Jesus.
24. Angels of death kill every deeply entrenched problem in my life in the name of Jesus.
25. Any power preparing coffin for my life, enter your coffin and die in the name of Jesus.

26. Evil programme in the heavens against my life scatter in the name of Jesus.
27. You the tree of non-achievement in my life be uprooted in the name of Jesus.
28. Household wickedness that has refused to let me go release me and die in the name of Jesus.
29. Any power that wants me to die unfulfilled die in the name of Jesus.
30. Evil priests ministering against my destiny be disgraced in the name of Jesus.
31. Evil altar fashioned against me scatter in the name of Jesus.
32. Every impossibility in any area of my life be destroyed in the name of Jesus.
33. God of Passover destroy every enemy of my joy in the name of Jesus.
34. I claim the freedom of Passover over the yoke of financial failure in the name of Jesus.
35. I release the plagues of Egypt into the camps of my enemies and I declare total freedom from oppositions to my breakthroughs in the name of Jesus.
36. Jesus has set me free, I cannot be bound and any power that refuses to let me go, die in the name of Jesus.
37. I thank the God of Passover for disgracing stubborn situations in my life in the name of Jesus.

# 21.

# *HEALING PRAYERS FOR THE SICK.*

*"And it came to pass, that the father of Publius lay sick of a fever and of a bloody flux: to whom Paul entered in, and prayed, and laid his hands on him, and healed him.*
*So when this was done, others also, which had diseases in the island, came, and were healed:"*

*Acts 28:8-9*

Sickness is not part of the scheme of God for His creation. Unfortunately, the conviction of many spiritually ignorant people, especially the medical folks is that sickness is caused by physical reasons only. Largely, sickness and disease are the ways that Satan rules the world. He enjoys afflicting as many people as possible and anytime that our Lord Jesus Christ healed the sick in the scriptures; He was directly destroying the completed works of darkness. In recent times, medical research has shown reliable evidence that healing prayers absolutely have positive consequences for the sick. This of course, had been the teachings of the Bible.

The Lord Jesus is still in the business of attacking and destroying the demons of sickness, healing the sick and undoing their damages. Jesus attributed some sicknesses to

the wickedness of the devil, in the book of Luke 13:10-13:
*"And he was teaching in one of the synagogues on the sabbath.*

*And, behold, there was a woman which had a spirit of infirmity eighteen years, and was bowed together, and could in no wise lift up herself.*

*And when Jesus saw her, he called her to him, and said unto her, Woman, thou art loosed from thine infirmity.*

*And he laid his hands on her: and immediately she was made straight, and glorified God."*

If you believe and have faith in the healing power of God to work in your vessel, deliverance will surely take place in your body through the powerful prayers in this segment. Whatever the ailment and whatever medical name it is given, prayer is the solution. By the power in the blood of Jesus, even cancer has answer. It is a wonderful thing to know that it is always the desire of our Lord Jesus Christ to set the captives free. Luke 5:12-13 *"And it came to pass, when he was in a certain city, behold a man full of leprosy: who seeing Jesus fell on his face, and besought him, saying, Lord, if thou wilt, thou canst make me clean.*

*And he put forth his hand, and touched him, saying, I will: be thou clean. And immediately the leprosy departed from him."*

Be expectant, the healing power of our Lord Jesus is about to flow into your body. It does not matter how long it takes; you must not stop praying and believing until you receive your healing.

**CONFESS THESE SCRIPTURES:**

**1 Peter 2:24:** Who his own self bare our sins in his own body on the tree, that we, being dead to sins, should live unto righteousness: by whose stripes ye were healed.

**Galatians 3:13-14:** Christ hath redeemed us from the curse of the law, being made a curse for us: for it is written, Cursed is every one that hangeth on a tree:

That the blessing of Abraham might come on the Gentiles through Jesus Christ; that we might receive the promise of the Spirit through faith.

**Matthew 8:16-17:** When the even was come, they brought unto him many that were possessed with devils: and he cast out the spirits with his word, and healed all that were sick:

That it might be fulfilled which was spoken by Esaias the prophet, saying, Himself took our infirmities, and bare our sicknesses.

**Matthew 9:35:** And Jesus went about all the cities and villages, teaching in their synagogues, and preaching the gospel of the kingdom, and healing every sickness and every disease among the people.

**Mark 3:10:** For he had healed many; insomuch that they pressed upon him for to touch him, as many as had plagues.

**Mark 5:25-29:** And a certain woman, which had an issue of blood twelve years,

And had suffered many things of many physicians, and had spent all that she had, and was nothing bettered, but rather grew worse,

When she had heard of Jesus, came in the press behind, and touched his garment.

For she said, If I may touch but his clothes, I shall be whole.

And straightway the fountain of her blood was dried up; and she felt in her body that she was healed of that plague.

**Mark 5:34:** And he said unto her, Daughter, thy faith hath made thee whole; go in peace, and be whole of thy plague.

## PRAYERS:

1. I soak myself in the blood of Jesus as I go into the healing prayers in the name of Jesus.
2. I believe the word of God that sets me free from any form of disease in the name of Jesus.
3. I believe the ability of the blood of Jesus to set me free from any form of affliction in the name of Jesus.
4. God, you are the source of all healing I wait upon you in the name of Jesus.
5. Father Lord, possess me by your power and let your Holy Spirit revive every organ of my body in the name of Jesus.
6. Lord Jesus I call upon you in my time of weakness and pain in the name of Jesus.
7. Lord Jesus, let your grace sustain me, and let not my strength and courage fail in the name of Jesus.
8. Father Lord, heal me and I will be healed in the name of Jesus.
9. Resurrection power of God, deliver me from the power of my enemies in the name of Jesus.
10. My Father, by your command, drive away from my body all sickness and infirmity in the name of Jesus.
11. O Lord, lay your calming hand upon me and let evil storm in my body cease in the name of Jesus.
12. Every demon of sickness in my body I bind you and cast you out in the name of Jesus.
13. I claim my healing by the stripes of our Lord Jesus Christ in the name of Jesus.

14. Evil curses working in my vessel die in the name of Jesus.

15. Lord Jesus, I touch the hem of your garment; release your deliverance power into my body in the name of Jesus.

16. What is impossible for the earthly physicians is possible for my creator; I claim my divine healing by the blood of Jesus.

17. Any satanic consumption in the dream affecting my life come out with your entire root and die in the name of Jesus.

18. By faith every plague of Egypt in my life die in the name of Jesus.

**Lay your right hand on any part of your body that you want the Lord to touch as you pray the next 7 prayers:**

19. Lord Jesus lay your hand on my body and let every troubler in my vessel die in the name of Jesus.

20. The Spirit of God that moved on creation move into my vessel in the name of Jesus.

21. Anything my Creator did not deposit in my body, be flushed out by the blood of Jesus.

22. You the demon attached to the sickness in my body I cast you out in the name of Jesus.

23. Let the power of Him that said, "Let there be light, and there was light" perform divine healing in my body in the name of Jesus.

24. Creative power of God form new parts in my vessel and make me whole in the name of Jesus.

25. By faith, I claim my divine healing in the name of Jesus.

**Pray the remaining prayers with holy violence:**

26. Every Pharaoh that has refused to let me go I declare your expiry in the name of Jesus.

27. I fire back every arrow of infirmity in the name of Jesus.
28. Satanic warrant officer enforcing bondage in my life, die in the name of Jesus.
29. I decree Passover over stubborn bondage in my life and I command you to die in the name of Jesus.
30. I reverse by fire any death sentence passed against my life in the name of Jesus.
31. Evil growths in my body wither from the root and be flushed out in the name of Jesus.
32. I break free from the grip of weakness and body pains in the name of Jesus.
33. Any infirmity in my life that is keeping me in bondage die in the name of Jesus.
34. Hands of darkness in my life be cut off in the name of Jesus.
35. By fire by force I rise up from the furnace of afflictions in the name of Jesus.
36. Witchcraft powers holding me in bondage release me and die in the name of Jesus.
37. The name of Jesus, that is above all names perform your miracle in my life in the name of Jesus.
38. I declare by faith my freedom from the demon of .............. *(name the sickness)* in the name of Jesus.
39. I declare by faith, I am no longer a candidate of ............... *(name the sickness)* in the name of Jesus.
40. I declare by faith, that the blood of Jesus has set me free from the demon of ................. *(name the sickness)* in the name of Jesus.
41. I claim my healing by faith in the name of Jesus.

# 22.

# *PRAYERS TO FULFILL DIVINE AGENDA.*

When God created man (male and female) in His own image in Genesis 26, it was for man to reign and have dominion over all other creations. God blessed man and said, *"Be fruitful, and multiply, and replenish the earth, and subdue it: and have dominion over the fish of the sea, and over the fowl of the air, and over every living thing that moveth upon the earth."*

When God looked at everything that He made he said, it was very good! If there are areas in your life that are not good, it is your responsibility to make it good again. The word of God says *"thou shall also decree a thing, and it shall be established unto thee."*

With the prayers you are going to pray here, you can bring new life to your destiny. The prayers will revive your dead destiny, for Jesus says, *"I am the resurrection, and life: he that believeth in me, though he were dead, yet shall he live:"*

**CONFESS THESE SCRIPTURES:**

**Isaiah 43:18-19:** Remember ye not the former things, neither consider the things of old. Behold, I will do a new thing; now it shall spring forth; shall ye not know it? I will even make a way in the wilderness, and rivers in the desert.

**Job 22:28:** Thou shalt also decree a thing, and it shall be established unto thee: and the light shall shine upon thy ways.

**John 11:25:** Jesus said unto her, I am the resurrection, and the life: he that believeth in me, though he were dead, yet shall he live:

**Ezekiel 37:1-10:** The hand of the LORD was upon me, and carried me out in the spirit of the LORD, and set me down in the midst of the valley which was full of bones,

And caused me to pass by them round about: and, behold, there were very many in the open valley; and, lo, they were very dry.

And he said unto me, Son of man, can these bones live? And I answered, O Lord GOD, thou knowest.

Again he said unto me, Prophesy upon these bones, and say unto them, O ye dry bones, hear the word of the LORD.

Thus saith the Lord GOD unto these bones; Behold, I will cause breath to enter into you, and ye shall live:

And I will lay sinews upon you, and will bring up flesh upon you, and cover you with skin, and put breath in you, and ye shall live; and ye shall know that I am the LORD.

So I prophesied as I was commanded: and as I prophesied, there was a noise, and behold a shaking, and the bones came together, bone to his bone.

And when I beheld, lo, the sinews and the flesh came up upon them, and the skin covered them above: but there was no breath in them.

Then said he unto me, Prophesy unto the wind, prophesy, son of man, and say to the wind, Thus saith the Lord GOD; Come from the four winds, O breath, and breathe upon these slain, that they may live.

So I prophesied as he commanded me, and the breath came into them, and they lived, and stood up upon their feet, an exceeding great army.

## PRAYERS:

1. My Father, do not ignore my cry in this prayer session in the name of Jesus.
2. Every tree of sorrow be uprooted in the name of Jesus.
3. Woe unto the vessel that the enemy is using to harm in the name of Jesus.
   **Lay your right hand on your head as you pray the following prayers:**
4. I fire back every arrow of the enemy, in the name of Jesus.
5. Every power that has stolen from my destiny return it and die in the name of Jesus.
   I refuse to serve my enemies, in the name of Jesus.
6. You the private enemy in my life, die in the name of Jesus.
7. Every good thing I have lost through satanic distraction and deception be returned by fire in the name of Jesus.
8. Sword of darkness meant to cut me down, turn back and destroy my enemies in the name of Jesus.

9. Furnace of affliction prepared for me, I command you by fire, envelope my enemies in the name of Jesus.

10. You the night that offers protection to my enemies, your loyalty has ended, turn against them in the name of Jesus.

11. Let the Pillar of fire that gives me light, give darkness to my detractors in the name of Jesus.

12. Lord, restore back onto me, everything I have lost to destiny pickpockects in the name of Jesus.

13. Any sin in me delaying my testimonies die in the name of Jesus.

14. Any power anywhere revoking the promises of God for my life die in the name of Jesus.

15. Satanic warrant officer assigned against my divine reward be disgraced in the name of Jesus.

16. My delayed benefits appear in the name of Jesus.

17. Holy Spirit, fertilise the womb of my life to give birth to my divine destiny in the name of Jesus.

18. Evil growths in my lot be roasted in the name of Jesus.

19. You the spiritual Lot in my divine allocation get out by fire in the name of Jesus.

20. Any resistance in the heavens against my joy scatter in the name of Jesus.

21. In the name of Jesus, nobody will say sorry to me or sorry about me.

22. Afflictions in my fortune die in the name of Jesus.

23. My divine rewards overshadow my life in the name of Jesus.

24. I receive power to overcome satanic violence in the name of Jesus.

25. Any power demanding my head on a pallet fall down and die in the name of Jesus.

26. Evil violence surrounding my life and destiny, scatter in the name of Jesus.
27. I fire back every arrow of wickedness fired into my destiny in the name of Jesus.
28. Evil storm in my divine inheritance be silenced in the name of Jesus.
29. Afflictions in my life, due to satanic violence die in the name of Jesus.
30. Satanic rage and imagination against my life scatter in the name of Jesus.
31. Any power anywhere revoking the promises of God for my life die in the name of Jesus.
32. You the house of war, waging against my house of peace die in the name of Jesus.
33. By fire by force, my life must go as it is written by God in the name of Jesus.
34. Any power that has manipulated my destiny, somersault and die in the name of Jesus.
35. Any evil hand that has ever stolen from me, wither by fire in the name of Jesus.
36. Every agenda of household wickedness for my destiny, scatter by fire in the name of Jesus.
37. Any power that wants to convert my destiny to rags, receive spiritual decay in the name of Jesus.
38. My vehicle of destiny shall reach its destination whether the enemy likes it or not in the name of Jesus.
39. Anything planted in my life to waste my destiny, come out with all your roots and die in the name of Jesus.
40. Any satanic driver in charge of the vehicle of my destiny be overthrown by the angels of the Living God in the name of Jesus.

41. Any power that wants me to come to the world in vain, die in the name of Jesus.
42. Satanic powers that had edited my divine destiny die by fire in the name of Jesus.
43. By the power in the blood of Jesus, I recover all that the enemies have stolen in my life from conception in the name of Jesus.
44. From now henceforth, I live to fulfil my divine destiny in the name of Jesus.

# Other Powerful Messages by the Author.

1. Fools in a snare.
2. The Mark of Sibboleth.
3. Evil in the House.
4. Fear Factor.
5. Dagger Vengeance.
6. Violence for Violence.
7. The enemy behind.
8. Believed Grasshoppers.
9. Down but not out.
10. Is it not in thy book?
11. I claim the impossible.
12. Making Jesus Vomit.
13. The anointing of Uzziah.
14. I refuse to give up.
15. Let God be God.
16. Look or Die.
17. Overcoming your Esau.
18. Overturn the Usual.
19. I come out!
20. Pay your due, claim your due.
21. My God get up!
22. Spoiling the treasures of darkness.
23. Step out of Shittim
24. Power over evil completion.
25. Power to feast before the enemies.
26. Power to fight from above.
27. Summon your power O God.
28. The battles you must win.
29. The hours of darkness.

30. The Lord's Job Advert.
31. The nature of the enemy.
32. The necessary concern.
33. The rod of the wicked.
34. Turning Northward.
35. Unlocking your destiny.
36. Victory against all odds.
37. The scale of balances.
38. When God gives up.
39. Overturning righteous verdicts.
40. Who are you?
41. The burden of inheritance.
42. Who is he that will harm you?
43. How can you sleep?
44. Knowing your stubborn enemies.
45. Revive us again.
46. The mystery of water.
47. The power of seven.
48. When they hear of your anointing.